Making polymer clay cards & tags

Jacqui Eccleson

GUILD OF MASTER CRAFTSMAN PUBLICATIONS LTD

First published 2004 by
Guild of Master Craftsman Publications Ltd
Castle Place, 166 High Street,
Lewes, East Sussex BN7 1XU

Text and illustrations © Jacqui Eccleson 2004
© in the work GMC Publications Ltd 2004
Photographs by Anthony Bailey, except the
photograph of the author on page 122
by Ronnie Eccleson

ISBN 1 86108 389 0

Publisher: Paul Richardson
Art Director: Ian Smith
Production Manager: Hilary MacCallum
Managing Editor: Gerrie Purcell
Project Editor: Dominique Page
Designer: Maggie Aldred

Colour origination by Icon Reprographics
Printed and bound by Sino Publishing House Ltd, Hong Kong, China

Measurements Notice
Although care has been taken to ensure that the imperial measurements are true and
accurate, they are only conversions from metric; they have been rounded up or down to
the nearest reasonable fraction of an inch. When following the projects, use either
the metric or the imperial measurements; do not mix units.

Making
polymer clay
cards & tags

Acknowledgements

In order to create the designs featured in this book, I purchased tools and materials from a wide variety of sources.

Since Fimo is my preferred working brand of polymer clay, I would like to take this opportunity to thank Staedtler (UK) Ltd.

Staedtler (UK) Ltd
Pontyclun
Rhondda Cynon Taff
CF72 8YJ
www.staedtler.com

Tel: +44 (0)1443 237421 for your nearest stockist of Fimo.

I would also like to acknowledge The Polymer Clay Pit, mail order suppliers of polymer clay and Kemper tool sets (specialized brass cutters).

The Polymer Clay Pit
3 Harts Lane
Wortham
Diss
Norfolk
IP22 1PQ
www.polymerclaypit.co.uk
Tel/Fax: +44 (0)1379 890176

The publishers would like to thank David Smith Contemporary Jewellery, Lewes, East Sussex for the loan of the gift box photographed with the *Be mine* tag on page 45, and Steamer Trading, Lewes, East Sussex for the loan of the pasta machine photographed on pages 15 and 18 and the cookie cutters pictured on pages 10, 13 and 16.

Contents

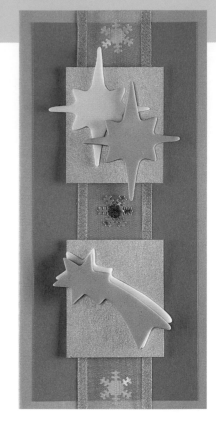

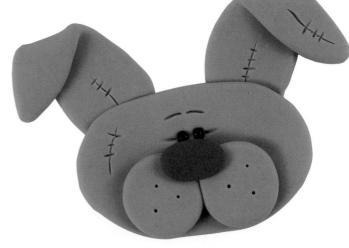

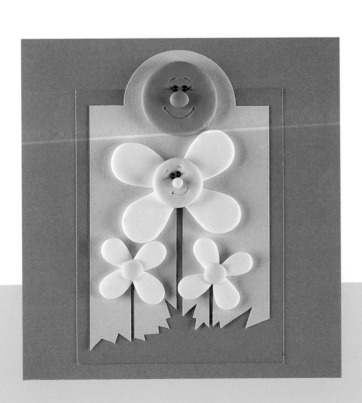

Introduction

If you, like me, appreciate gift ideas with a difference, you
are sure to enjoy the combination of clay modelling and paper craft
within the contents of this book. The designs are bright and
all the modelled pieces are easily created.

Whether you are a complete novice to the craft or just simply
seeking inspiration to aid card-making, you will find all the projects
achievable. Each design is adaptable and suitable for a multitude
of occasions. A printed insert can even transform a proposed
greeting card into an invitation – the choice is entirely yours!

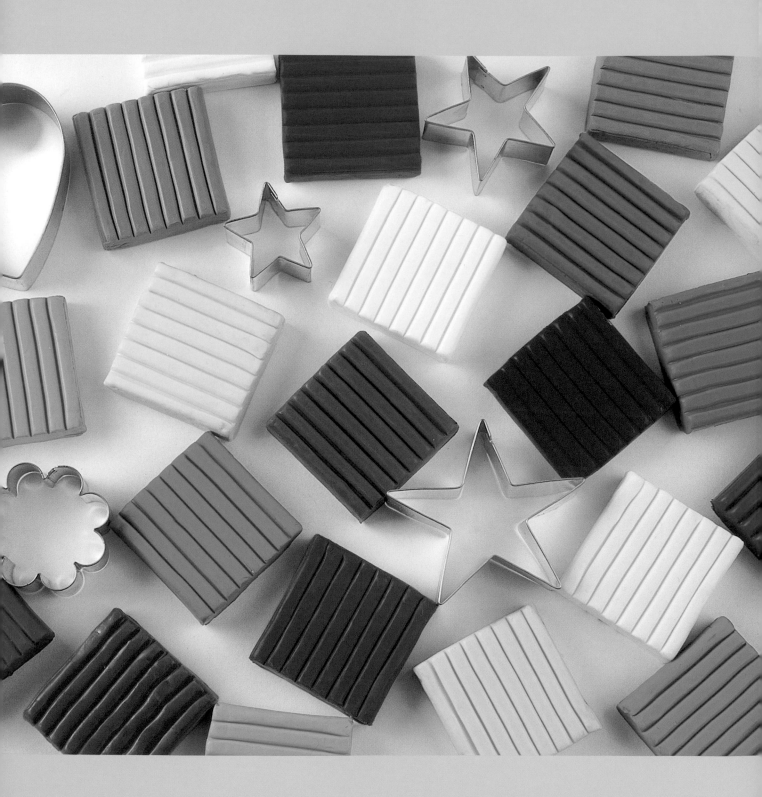

Materials and equipment

Clay

Polymer clay is available in a few brand names but I personally prefer Fimo, as it tends to keep better form – no detail is lost even after baking. The clay is available in Classic form and a Soft variety. Both can be mixed together and work in perfect harmony. The Classic variety requires a little more conditioning, though.

Paper and cards

Card blanks, matching envelopes, coloured paper and card can all be purchased from craft and stationery outlets. Matching cards and envelopes are often bought in packs but some retailers supply them separately. Sheets of corrugated card are available as single sheets and can be quite costly. However, a tool known as a Ribbler or, more commonly, a paper crimper will enable you to create your own corrugated paper or card, if you prefer.

Please note that for some of the projects I stipulate the use of A6 and DL card sizes. The measurements for these are as follows: A6 = 6in x 4^1/$_8$ in (148mm x 105mm) and DL = 8^1/$_4$in x 4in (210mm x 100mm).

A wide choice of coloured paper and card is available from craft and stationery outlets

A selection of card blanks

Use a paper crimper to create your own corrugated paper or card

Paper trimmers

If your budget allows, a trimmer is a worthwhile cutting aid, and you may feel more comfortable using a trimmer rather than a craft knife. They are available in a range of sizes, and their size determines their price. Small trimmers are reasonably inexpensive.

Metal ruler

Plastic rulers are fine for measurement alone but a metal ruler is advisable when cutting. Some metal rulers have a moulded safety bar, which is important as scalpels or craft knives can slip across rulers, risking fingers being cut. Care is essential.

When incorporating polymer clay into your card-making, colour-matched envelopes are fine, as long as you are personally presenting the card. Posting any polymer project will require the added protection of a padded envelope. These are widely available in an assortment of sizes. Shallow boxes made to protect handmade cards are also available from craft stores. It's worth knowing your efforts are not going to be wasted on arrival!

Propelling pencil

When marking measurements in pencil on paper or card it's easier to mark accurately with a propelling pencil.

Cutting aids

Scalpel and cutting mat

I tend to use a scalpel and a self-healing cutting mat. The mat provides a rigid work surface and protects your worktable. Cutting mats also have printed grids on the surface, which can be useful when cutting paper and card at right angles.

A variety of envelopes

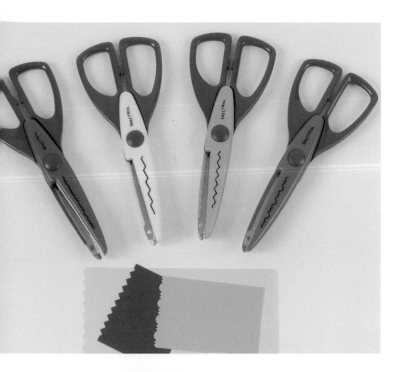

Scissors

When cutting any traced templates from the book, it's often easier to cut them out with scissors. Curved cosmetic or craft scissors are handy for cutting any awkward, curvy areas. Decorative craft scissors can be used to create fancy borders and enhance card edges.

Cutters

Your craft knife or scalpel will be constantly used for dividing clay into equal amounts and cutting around templates transferred onto rolled clay. Cookie cutters are an additional cutting aid.

safety **advice**
● Ensure that cookie cutters are only used for clay and never considered for food preparation at a later date.

Top: Decorative craft scissors
Above: Useful cutting and measuring aids
Right: Cookie cutters come in a range of shapes and sizes and are great for using with polymer clay

Specific clay cutters can be purchased from craft stores. Kemper tools (see acknowledgements) manufacture small brass cutters with spring-loaded plungers that come in various shapes and sizes. Small metal cutters are also available from stores specializing in sugar paste and cake decoration. Purchase a variety of cutters to add valuable tools to your toolbox.

Small brass cutters, specially designed for use with clay

Modelling tools

Special tools can be bought for shaping or sculpting clay. Use what you feel comfortable with. In my opinion, your own hands are the perfect modelling tool. Small items like cocktail sticks and pins are ideal for scratching the surface of the clay, making indents or holes where required.

Craft adhesives

PVA (Polyvinyl acetate)

PVA is available in many brand names. This is multipurpose glue that dries clear, making it ideal when applying paper and card to your designs. An alternative would be to use double-sided tape, but this is a more expensive option. PVA can also be used to fix baked clay to card. Use a brand that ensures a rapid bond. I've tried a few adhesives with clay and found that Sobo Premium craft glue gave the best results.

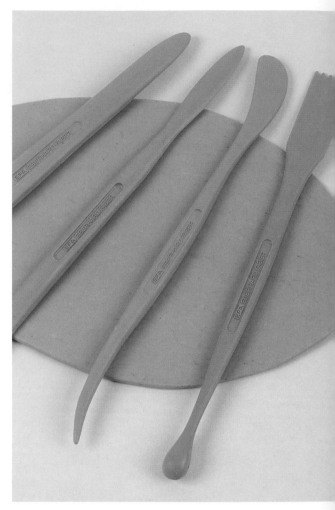

Tools for sculpting clay

Instant adhesive (cyanoacrylate)

I often use an instant adhesive when fixing clay parts to my projects. As its name suggests, there is virtually no drying time.

Some of these products are now available in a bottle housing a small brush, making it easy to apply the glue to tiny clay parts. Make sure you only use very small amounts, though, as the glue tends to spread on contact with paper or card, and too much can cause staining around any fixed modelled parts. This, of course, would spoil the look of any project.

3-D foam pads

Double-sided sticky foam pads are great for card-making. They are clean and easy to use and also add dimension to your designs.

useful tips

• Adding too much glue to any paper or card can cause it to wrinkle or warp. Use it sparingly and apply with a spreader to ensure even coverage. A piece of rigid card will serve the purpose.

• If working with an instant adhesive, hold small project parts with tweezers. Positioning is made easier and it prevents the glue from making contact with your skin.

• It's always best to use a glue that you are familiar with.

safety advice

• Care is essential when working with instant adhesive glue. Avoid contact with eyes or skin and work in a well-ventilated room, as fumes can be omitted.

Adhesives, double-sided tape and foam pads

Rollers

As the clay can stick to surfaces, you will need a non-stick roller. Your toolbox may already contain a roller in the form of anything from a printer's roller, an acrylic brayer or a metal/plastic rod, any of which would be suitable.

I recently purchased a pasta machine, making rolling a lot easier. I found it even cut down on the amount of air bubbles being produced.

Left: Pasta machine and non-stick roller

Tips and techniques

Baking

It's a good idea to find a suitable work and baking surface before beginning a clay project. Something like a small melamine dinner tray is ideal for working your clay. When baking, it is important to use a flat, rigid surface to ensure flatness to each modelled piece. I use a ceramic tile, which is safe to place in the oven, as the baking temperature is very low. A rigid baking tray lined with baking parchment or aluminium foil may be used as an alternative.

Ovens can vary in temperature, making an oven thermometer a sound investment. That way you will be sure to follow the recommended temperature for the product. Fimo, my preferred clay, requires 30 minutes at 265°F/130°C.

Place your work on the middle shelf of the oven. After baking is complete, remove and allow the

clay to cool. The clay hardens during the cooling process, so don't be too hasty in removing projects from the baking surface.

Small ovens may be purchased for the sole use of your craft, but the home oven suits most people.

A ceramic tile can be used as a baking surface. Use an oven thermometer to ensure the correct temperature

Hygiene and safety

As a precautionary step I would suggest you clean your oven after baking polymer clay. Bicarbonate of soda mixed with water is a simple yet effective cleaning solution.

Anyone who has worked with polymer clay before will have noticed that deposits of colour can be left on your hands, so I recommend that you wash your hands each time you are about to use a different colour, especially if modelling dark colours then continuing to model with a lighter-coloured clay. Soap and a soft nailbrush will ensure removal of any colour deposit. Having baby wipes close to hand may be more convenient. Colour deposits can also build up on your work area and are easily cleaned with a little water and a paper towel.

Clay conditioning

All clay should be well worked or kneaded before use. Without doing so, the product won't work for you as intended. The heat of your hands will quickly break the clay down to a more malleable consistency. Alternate rolling, folding and pressing with fingers will soon soften the product but avoid working it to a sticky consistency. If using the Classic variety of Fimo, please note that it needs a little more conditioning than the Soft variety.

Rolling

Clay rolled thin can stick to a work surface if continuously rolled without lifting and turning, so you will need to use a non-stick roller. Alternatively, a pasta machine will make the process easier and help cut down on the amount of air bubbles being produced. Should this problem arise when hand rolling, prick the air bubbles with a pin and gently press the area with your finger. Finally, use a roller to push the bubbled areas to the outer edges.

A pasta machine or non-stick roller will make rolling polymer clay easier

Marbling

You can create some wonderful effects by marbling clay, just follow these four simple steps:

1 Condition the clay, ensuring that each colour you intend to use is of the same consistency. Equal amounts of each colour are not necessary.

2 Roll each colour into a cylinder.

3 Line the colours up side by side and then twist together to start the mixing.

4 The clay can now be rolled, folded and twisted again. Stop when the desired effect is achieved.

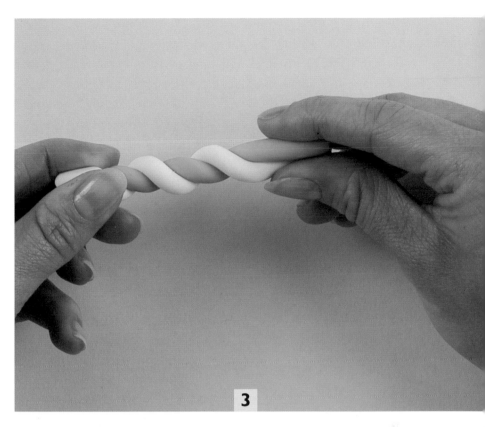

3

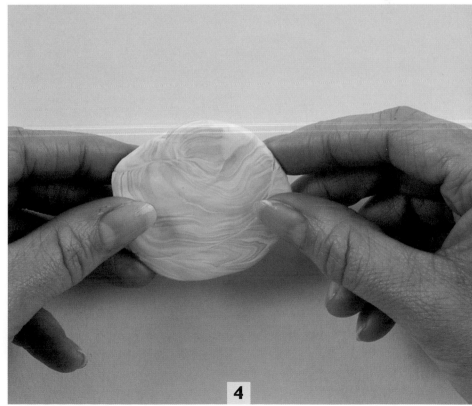

4

Top right: Twisted clay ready for marbling
Right: Marbled clay

Measuring clay

Most of the modelled pieces featured in this book start with a ball of clay rolled to a specific diameter. The easiest way to do this is to pull off small pieces of clay from the block, condition them, roll to a ball and place a ruler in front to gauge the diameter. Add or subtract small amounts until the required amount is obtained. Everyone's judgement is different and, obviously, small differences are acceptable and will not create noticeable results. However, it's always better to have a slightly lesser quantity to avoid the baked clay adding too much weight to the finished card.

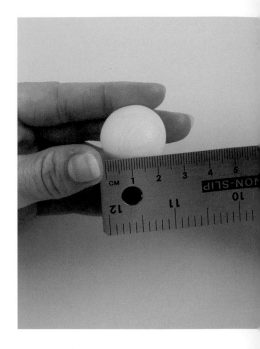

Tracing onto clay

Any project that requires a template shape to be cut from clay couldn't be easier:

1 Trace the required template onto white paper.

2 Roll enough clay or the said quantity to a depth of $1/16$in (2mm).

3 Equip yourself with a sewing needle or pin. Place the tracing directly onto the clay's surface and use the desired tool to trace the shape by applying gentle pressure to the outline.

useful tips

● When marbling, avoid pressing and smearing the clay, as it tends to result in mixed, muddy colours.

● Take care of your tools by removing any clay residue from cutting edges. You can wipe the edges with a paper towel or wash in warm water and dry thoroughly.

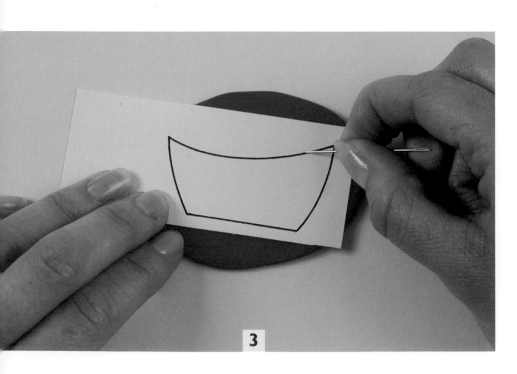

Above: Measuring the diameter of a ball of clay
Left: Tracing a template onto clay

4 An impression of the shape will be visible on the surface of the clay.

5 Using a cutting mat, carefully cut out the marked area with your craft knife.

Adding inserts to cards

Each card design within the book can, if desired, be completed with an added insert. Make sure you choose a good-quality paper (90–100g) and decide whether you want to make a folded or a single-sheet insert. No matter what your preference is, the insert should be cut slightly smaller than the card itself. By following this advice your insert will remain within the borders of the card when it is closed.

Folded inserts can be secured to the inside back card with a little double-sided tape or glue placed alongside the fold. Apply a small amount of tape or glue to the top of a single-sheet insert to secure.

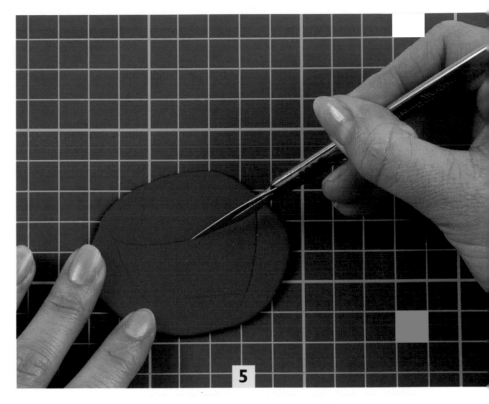

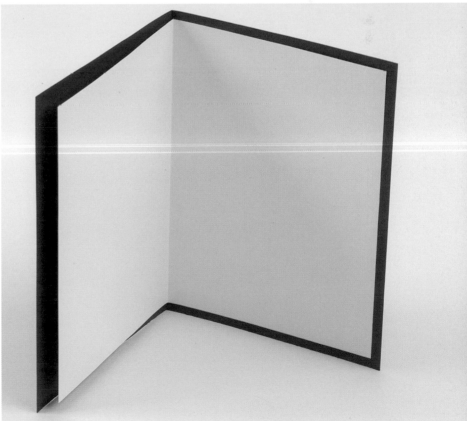

Top right: Cutting the traced outline with a craft knife
Right: Card with insert

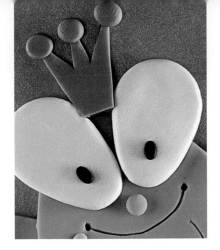

New home

MATERIALS AND EQUIPMENT

- White pearlescent card blank
  – 5in (125mm) sq.
- Pearlescent blue paper
- Dark green paper or
  lightweight card
- White paper
- Tracing paper
- Black permanent pen (fine nib)
- Ruler
- Craft knife
- Pin
- Non-stick roller
- Strong glue
- Double-sided tape
- Scissors
- Clay cutter – 1/2in (13mm)
  teardrop
- Polymer clay (Fimo): apple green,
  white, black, golden yellow, ochre,
  red, pacific blue

Create this delightful character hopping to his new pad and send wishes to someone starting anew.

Prepare the card

1 Cut a square from pearlescent blue paper that is slightly smaller than the card blank. Use double-sided tape to fix the square in a central position to the front of the card.

2 Trace the lily-pad template (A), provided on page 115, onto dark green paper or card of your choice. Cut out and paste to the base of your card.

3 Use a fine-nib black pen to draw small, delicate dragonfly wings onto white paper. Use scissors to cut out the wings and then apply small beads of glue to the reverse and position them at an angle at the top of the card.

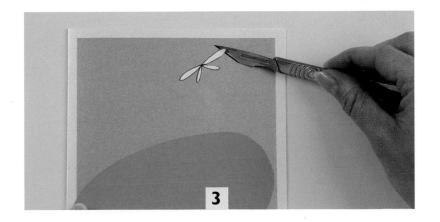

Frog's body and rear legs

4 Condition half a block of apple green Fimo. Roll the clay with a non-stick roller or desired tool to a depth of 1/16in (2mm), ensuring that the clay is free of air pockets. (See *useful tip* on page 27.)

5 Trace the leg and body templates (B and C, page 115) and refer to *Tips and techniques*, *Tracing onto clay*, pages 20–21. Enhance the body by defining the frog's forelegs. Score the clay with a pin to outline the area. Define the mouth in the same way.

6 Place the hind-leg shape onto a suitable baking surface and carefully position the body part on top. Create several tiny yellow clay balls and place them at random on the frog's body. Gently press each one flat with your finger to fix their position.

Eyes and nose

7 For the eyes, roll a 5/8in (15mm) ball of white clay. Split the quantity in half with your knife then re-roll each piece into a ball. Flatten each ball and shape into a rounded drop. Stretch the clay to elongate. Set the eyes at an angle at the top of the head.

8 Make tiny black oval pupils and fix them to the base of each eye, pressing them gently in place. Add a small ball of green clay for the nose.

8

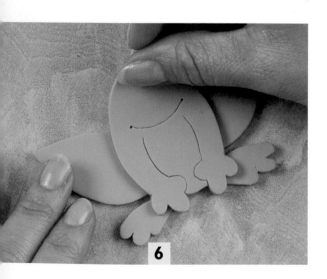

6

Crown

9 Roll out a small piece of ochre clay. Measure the space between the eyes to give you the width of the crown's base. Cut out a simple three-point crown shape. Fix the crown onto the head and decorate with jewels (three little clay balls).

Dragonfly

10 A ³/₁₆in (5mm) ball of pacific blue clay will be enough to form two body parts and a head. Roll the small ball into a thin log that is 1³/₈in (35mm) long. Remove a ¹/₄in (6mm) length to form a small capsule-like body segment. Remove another small piece to make a ball-shaped head. Shape the large body segment from the remainder.

Water lily

11 Roll out a small amount of white clay. Use a teardrop cutter to form three petal shapes. Alternatively, create small discs and shape them by pinching the outer edges into a point. Assemble the petals as shown, with a small pink ball added to the centre.

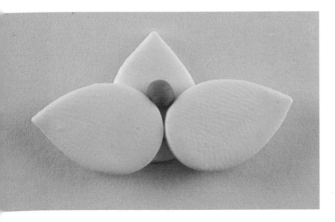

Bake

12 Place the modelled clay parts onto a suitable baking surface. Bake the Fimo at 265°F/130°C for 30 minutes. (Follow the manufacturer's instructions if using a different brand of clay.) Allow ample cooling time.

Assemble

13 Carefully remove from the baking surface. Position the clay pieces in a pleasing composition and secure with strong glue. With a black permanent pen, add small dots to depict a jumping motion from the watery background to the pad.

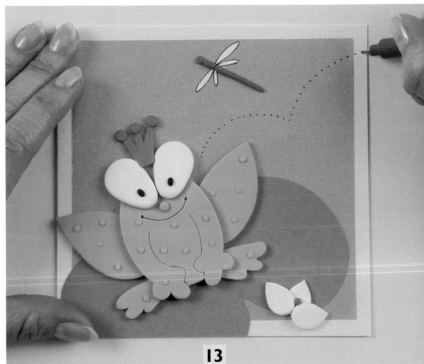

useful tip

● If your clay develops air pockets during the rolling process, prick the air bubbles with a pin and gently press the area with your finger. Use a roller to push the bubbled areas to the outer edges.

Darting dwellers

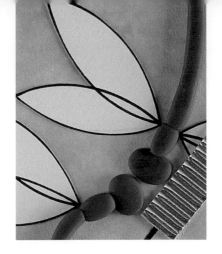

MATERIALS AND EQUIPMENT

- A6 silver card blank
- Marlmarque (marble) blue paper
- White card
- Bright blue card
- Gold corrugated card
- Black pigment liner 0.5
  (permanent pen)
- Pencil
- Ruler
- Craft knife
- Tracing paper
- Strong glue
- Double-sided tape
- Polymer clay (Fimo): pacific blue

Design a card that features an appealing composition: a combination of cool silver and blues warmed with gold and enhanced by the dazzling beauty of dragonflies.

Prepare the card

The full-size illustration on page 115 shows a background block of 2⁵/₈in (65mm) wide x 3¹/₄in (85mm) deep with a joining rectangle of 3³/₄in (95mm) wide x 1⁵/₈in (40mm) deep to the base. Mark these measurements onto bright blue card, cut out and refer to the illustration for positioning. Secure it to the silver card blank with glue or double-sided tape.

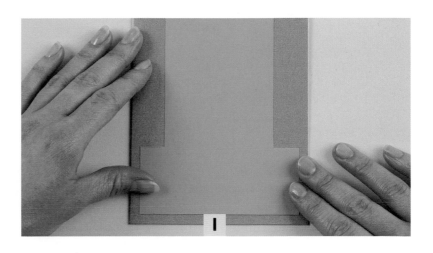

2

2 Cut out a marbled blue paper rectangle to fit within the upper section of the bright blue panel then secure it in the same way.

3 Create the stems by carefully marking two curved lines onto the card with a black pen.

4 Use the wings in the illustration on page 115 as templates. Trace and transfer them onto white card then outline each with black pen and cut out. Fix into position as shown.

5 Cut out rectangles that measure 2¹/₄in (55mm) x ³/₈in (10mm) and 1¹/₈in (30mm) x ⁵/₁₆in (8mm) from a piece of gold corrugated card to form the bulrush heads. Secure to the stems with double-sided tape or glue.

Dragonflies

6 From a block of pacific blue clay, remove the following quantities and divide each into two equal parts.

Head	¹/₄in (6mm) diameter ball to form two flat ovals
Thorax	¹/₄in (6mm) diameter ball to form two small flat capsule shapes
Abdomen	¹/₂in (13mm) diameter ball to form two flat tapered logs that are 2in (50mm) long

7 On your work surface, carefully join the pieces together to assemble each dragonfly. A gentle curve will bring life to each stick-like body.

Bake

8 Bake the dragonflies on a suitable surface. Allow sufficient time for cooling.

Assemble

9 Carefully remove the modelled parts from the baking surface and glue them in position on the card.

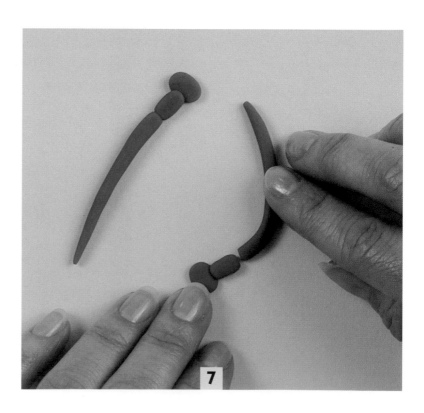

7

Heart of gold

MATERIALS AND EQUIPMENT

- A6 cream card blank
- Gold card or paper
- Burgundy card or paper
- Gold corrugated card
- Gold lamé ribbon – approx. ¹/₂in
  (13mm) width
- Pencil
- Ruler
- Pin
- Tracing paper
- Craft knife
- Strong PVA glue
- Double-sided tape
- Sticky foam pads
- Small heart craft punch
- Polymer clay (Fimo): gold

Designed for you to recreate with love, deservedly for someone who has a heart of gold.

Prepare the card

1 Cut two pieces of ribbon, slightly longer than the length of the card. Use a pencil to lightly mark a 1in (25mm) margin to the left side of the card and glue the ribbons with a small gap between each. Fold and secure the excess to the inner front of the card.

2 Tear a piece of gold card measuring approximately 2in (50mm) wide x 3in (75mm) deep, then tear a piece of burgundy card to fit within. Glue these pieces together and position them towards the top of the card.

1

Bake

6 With the technique applied and the shape cut, bake the clay heart at the recommended time and temperature. Allow time for the clay to cool.

Assemble

7 Use a strong PVA to fix the heart in an offset position to the layered card. Attach the mounted gold heart to its centre to complete the project.

3 Cut three thin strips of gold corrugated card measuring 1³/₈in (35mm) long. Glue two strips horizontally with an overlap to the left of the layered card. Fix the remaining strip to the right side, ³/₈in (10mm) from the base. Use glue or double-sided tape to secure. Glue a small rectangular piece of torn gold card above the corrugated strip to the base.

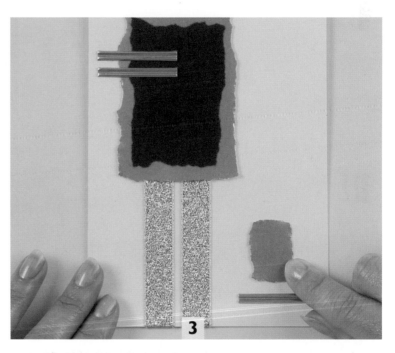

4 Cut a ³/₄in (20mm) square of burgundy card. Use a craft punch to create a small heart from gold card. Mount the heart on the square with a small piece of sticky foam pad. Fix another sticky pad to the reverse of the square. Keep this piece for the final assembly.

Heart

5 Roll some gold clay to a depth of ¹/₁₆in (2mm). Make sure you have enough to accommodate the heart template on page 116. Refer to *Tips and techniques*, *Tracing onto clay*, pages 20–21, for transferring the image.

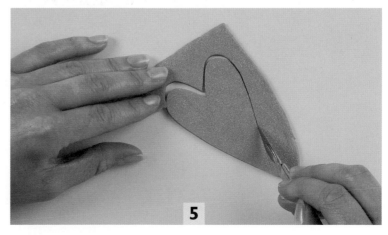

New arrival

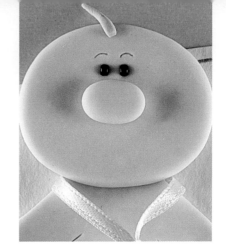

MATERIALS AND EQUIPMENT

- A6 pearlescent green card blank
- Yellow card
- Pale green card
- Paper
- Ruler
- Pencil
- Eraser
- Pin
- Cocktail stick
- Green coloured pencil
- Sticky foam pads
- Strong glue
- Black seed beads
- Baby blue ribbon – 1/8in
  (3mm) width
- Decorative silver plastic dummy
- Polymer clay (Fimo): flesh pink,
  golden yellow, white, orange,
  sahara, pastel mint, pastel lemon

Celebrate the arrival of a new life.
This charming design can be adapted
to suit the gender of the newborn baby.

Prepare the card

1 The patch-like panels are easily formed by marking out rectangles that measure 3 1/2in (90mm) x 3in (75mm) and 2 3/8in (60mm) x 2 1/4in (55mm) onto yellow card. Use a pencil to add subtle curves to the measured areas and cut out.

2 Draw a 1 5/8in (40mm) square panel onto pale green card and cut it in the same way. Erase any pencil marks.

3 Use a green pencil to mark each corner with a small dot. Continue by marking small stitches at the edges of each patch.

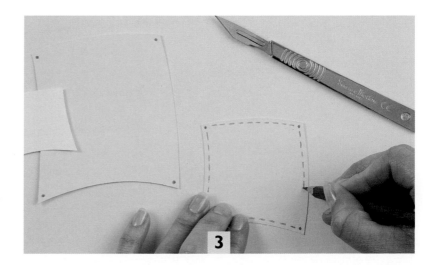

3

4 Glue the largest yellow patch to the card at an angle. To the left side, fix the green patch on top.

5 Create random stitching from the patches onto the card using your green coloured pencil.

6 On the reverse of the remaining patch, apply sticky pads to three corners. This piece will be used in the final stages of the design.

Baby's head

7 Make this from a flesh-pink clay ball with an 11/16in (17mm) diameter. Gently flatten the ball between your thumbs and forefingers, creating a disc. Keep turning the clay to ensure equal pressure all round. Stretch the clay to a width of 1 3/8in (35mm).

8 Take a very small amount of sahara-coloured clay and roll it into a tapered log. Place it at the top of the head, giving the baby a wisp of hair.

9 Make a small flesh-coloured oval and place it at the halfway position on the head to create a nose then insert two beads above for eyes. Scratch the clay with a pin to add little eyebrows.

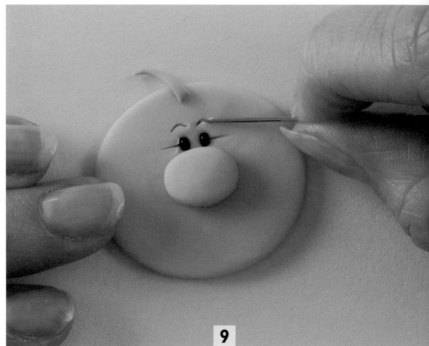

Baby's body

10 A 1in (25mm) ball of the same colour is ample for the body. Roll the clay to a thickness of 1/16in (2mm). Trace the body template on page 116 onto paper and place the tracing onto the clay. With a needle or pin, trace around the body outline and arm detail.

11 Remove the tracing to reveal a transferred outline on the clay's surface. Cut around the shape. Score into the clay with a pin to enhance the arms and little fingers.

12 Gently flatten 3/16in (5mm) of clay at the top of the neckline. This will enable the head to sit flush with the body. Attach the head.

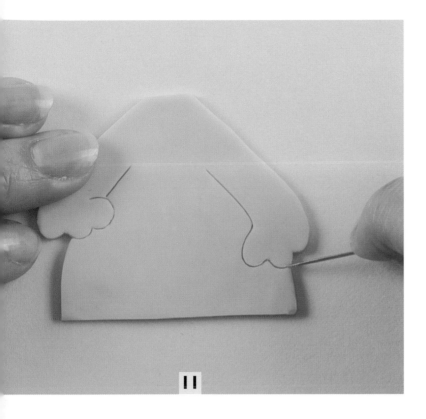

11

Duckling

13 Mix some white clay with a lesser quantity of golden yellow to create a soft yellow. (Use a manufactured colour if preferred.) Form the duck's head from a 3/8in (10mm) ball of clay, flattened to a disc that has a 5/8in (15mm) diameter.

14 A 1/2in (13mm) ball of clay will form the body. Shape the ball into another disc and bend into a crescent moon shape. Attach the head to the body.

15 Create a teardrop-shaped wing from a 1/4in (6mm) ball of the same colour. Curve the shape to suit. Make two cuts with a craft knife to add detail and complete the wing.

16 Finish the duck's head by creating a small orange triangle for its beak and insert a bead for its eye.

17 Now carefully attach the duck to the bottom left side of the baby's body.

Buttons

18 Roll a 5/16in (8mm) ball of pastel lemon and a 3/8in (10mm) ball of pastel mint clay. Divide each quantity into two equal parts. Shape them into discs then use a cocktail stick to make little holes in each button. Join two buttons together.

Bake

19 Place all the modelled pieces onto your chosen baking surface and bake at the manufacturer's recommendation. Allow time for cooling.

Assemble

20 Cut approximately 4in (100mm) of ribbon and loop it through the plastic dummy. Hang the ribbon from the neck area and secure the ends to the back of the body with a little glue. Strong, fast-drying glue applied to the body and head will secure the piece to your card. Affix the yellow patch, covering a small section of the duckling and baby's body. Buttons can be placed in the position of your choice and secured with the same adhesive.

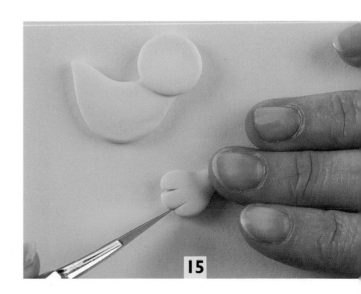

15

Tiny toes

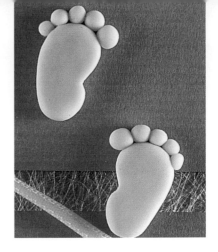

MATERIALS AND EQUIPMENT

- A6 cream card blank
- Pale blue card
- White angel hair
- Ruler
- Pencil
- Craft knife
- Cocktail stick
- Tweezers
- Ribbon – 1/8in (3mm) width
- Small single-hole punch
- Strong craft glue
- Polymer clay (Fimo): flesh pink

For the matching gift tag:

- Blue card
- Cream card
- Cream ribbon – 1/8in (3mm) width
- Small single-hole punch
- Cocktail stick
- Polymer clay (Fimo): flesh pink,
  peppermint blue, white

A quick and simple card to make that welcomes the patter of tiny feet. Shades of pink could replace the blues to be more appropriate for a baby girl.

Prepare the card

1 Open the A6 card in order to punch holes in the front only. Position the hole punch approximately 3/4in (20mm) from the base of the card and punch a small hole to the right side of the fold line. Turn the card and repeat for a second hole.

2 Create a layered background for the card. Start with a blue card rectangle that is 2 3/4in (70mm) wide x 3 1/4in (85mm) deep.

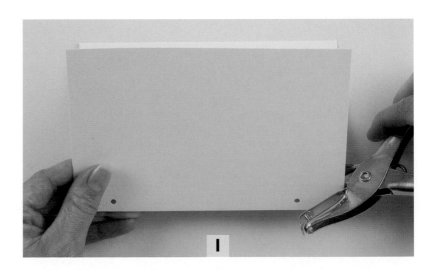

3 Cut a rectangular piece of white angel hair to fit within. Use tiny beads of glue to secure. Finish with a smaller blue card rectangle glued to the centre. Fix the layered panel ³/₈in (10mm) from the top of the card in a central position.

4 Cut enough ribbon to enable you to tie a bow after threading. Feed the ribbon through the back of each hole and tie at the front of the card. Apply a small amount of glue to the tied area and hold in position until secure. Continue by creating a bow, cutting the ribbon ends to suit. Glue applied to the bow's knot will prevent it from coming undone.

Feet

5 Roll a ball of flesh pink clay that has a diameter that is approximately ¹¹/₁₆in (17mm). Divide it into six equal parts. Form six discs and mould each one into a rounded teardrop shape.

6 Take three shaped parts and indent each with a cocktail stick on the right side and repeat on the left for the remaining three. Gently smooth over the indents with your finger, removing any sharpness. Providing the clay was divided equally, each foot should be of a similar size.

7 Make little ball-like toes, decreasing in size towards the outer edge of the foot. Gently press the toes into position to complete each one.

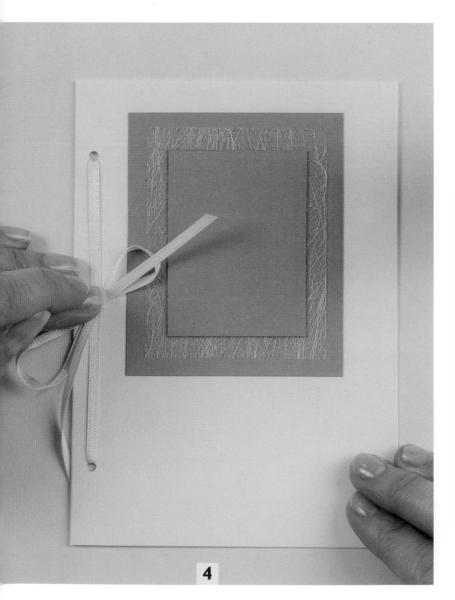

4

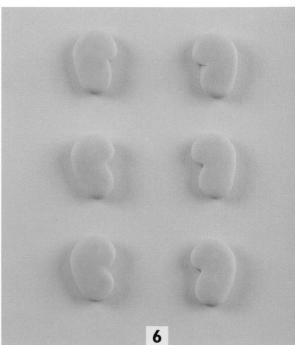

6

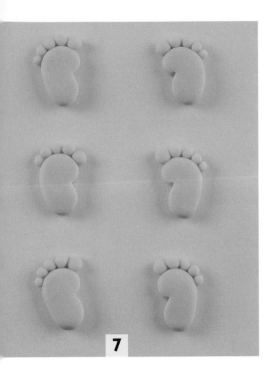

7

Bake

8 Bake the clay feet at the manufacturer's recommendation for the product and then allow the clay to cool.

Assemble

9 Lay the feet on the card, leaving a 3/8in (10mm) margin at the base. Arrange them, creating tiny steps through the centre of the card. Fix the position of each small foot.

---

useful **tip**

• Tweezers can be used to hold each foot when applying the glue.

Matching **tag**

1 Cut a 3in (75mm) square from blue card. Cut away the corners and then punch a hole in the top and bottom on one side.

2 Cut a 2³/8in (60mm) square of cream card. Fix to the centre of the blue tag using glue or double-sided tape.

3 Create the central panel from a 2in (50mm) square of blue card and a slightly smaller square of cream card on top. Secure both to the centre of the tag at an angle.

4 Create the small feet in the same way as for the card project.

5 Make pale blue buttons from two equal-sized balls of clay, flattened into small discs. Use a cocktail stick to add detail and then bake the clay.

7 Add a message to the back of the tag before finally gluing the clay embellishments to the front.

8 Feed a piece of ribbon through the punched holes and tie in a bow.

Be mine

MATERIALS AND EQUIPMENT

- DL-sized burgundy card blank
- Gold card
- Pink paper
- Decorative craft scissors
- Small heart craft punch
- Clay cutter – ¹/₂in (13mm) heart
- Strong glue
- Double-sided tape
- Sticky foam pads
- Craft knife
- Pencil
- Ruler
- Polymer clay (Fimo): red, white

For the matching gift tag:

- Card in gold, burgundy and pink
- Sticky foam pad
- Burgundy ribbon – ¹/₈in
  (3mm) width
- Gold ribbon – ¹/₈in (3mm) width
- Small single-hole punch
- Clay cutter – ¹/₂in (13mm) heart
- Polymer clay (Fimo): red, white

Roses are always a romantic gesture.
Add to the romance with this lovingly
created card.

Prepare the card

1 Mark a faint pencil line from the top to the bottom of the card, ³/₈in (10mm) from the opening edge. Open the card and cut away this strip using decorative scissors.

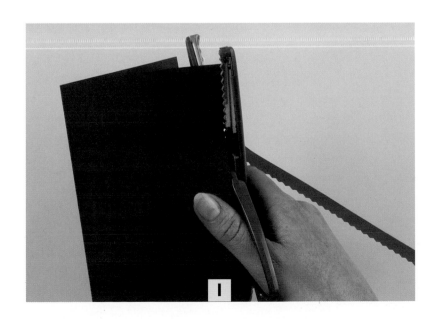

2

2 Cut a single-leaf insert from pink paper to fit within the card. Use a craft punch to punch out a heart shape at the centre base of the insert. Secure the insert at the top of the card with a small strip of double-sided tape.

3 On gold card, measure and cut out three rectangles that are 1 5/8in (40mm) wide x 2in (50mm) deep. Use a craft punch to remove a heart shape from the base of one rectangle. Keep the punched shape for later use.

4 Fix sticky pads to the back of the gold rectangles. Position the first gold panel 3/8in (10mm) from the top of the card. Leave the same margin at the base when positioning the punched panel. Centre the remaining gold panel.

Pink roses

5 Mix a little red clay to white to create pink. Mix enough to form an 11/16in (17mm) ball. (You may want to use a manufactured colour instead of your own mix.) Roll the quantity into a log that is approximately 4in (100mm) long and divide it into four equal parts.

6 Squeeze one of the four pieces of clay flat between your fingers. Lay the clay on your work surface and cut it in half with a knife. Working from the cut edge, roll each piece inward to form a coiled roll. This will create two rose centres.

7 Pick up another pink part and divide it into eight equal amounts. These little sections are used to create the petals (four petals to each rose). To do so, roll each small piece into a ball and flatten between your thumb and forefinger. Press the discs around the two rose centres created earlier.

8 When the petals are positioned, roll the heavy base of the rose between your fingers into a stem and then cut away the excess. You will be left with a flat-backed rose head. Repeat to give a total of four pink roses.

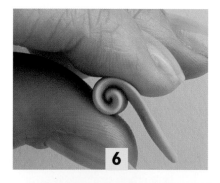

6

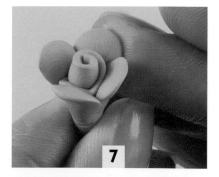

7

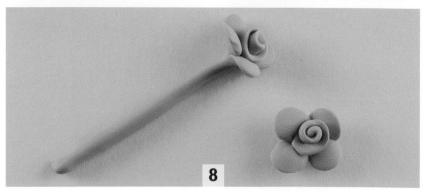

8

Hearts

9 The excess clay is more than enough to create two pink hearts. Gather the clay together and roll out until it is $^1/_{16}$in (2mm) thick. Use a heart-shaped clay cutter.

Red roses

10 Use a $^1/_2$in (13mm) ball of clay to form the red roses. Roll to a log length of 2in (50mm). Divide into two equal parts. Start by flattening one part then cut in half with a knife. The method is the same as for the pink roses. Follow the instructions to create two red roses.

11 On a flat work surface, join the roses together in pairs with petals overlapping. Place two pinks together, leaving you with a red/pink mix for the remaining pairs.

Bake

12 Bake all the modelled parts on a suitable baking surface. Allow time for cooling.

Assemble

13 Position the clay pieces as follows and then fix them with strong craft glue:

Top rectangle   Vertically – red/pink
Middle rectangle   Diagonally – pink
Bottom rectangle   Horizontally – pink/red

14 The punched-out gold heart from the base rectangle can now be glued between the top and middle gold rectangles on the card. Glue the two clay hearts between the middle and base gold rectangle.

Matching tag

1 Cut a piece of gold card measuring $2^3/_8$in (60mm) wide x 4in (100mm) deep. Use a hand-held punch to make a single hole in the centre top.

2 Tape or glue a burgundy card rectangle measuring $1^5/_8$in (40mm) wide x $2^3/_4$in (70mm) deep to the top left and a pink panel measuring $1^1/_8$in (30mm) wide x $3^1/_8$in (80mm) deep to the bottom right corner. Add a message of your choice.

3 Cut a 1in (25mm) square from gold card and fix a sticky foam pad to the reverse. Mount the square to overlap the layered panels.

4 Create a clay rose, as for the card project, and use a cutter to create the heart. Bake the clay.

5 Glue the rose to the centre of the gold square and the heart to the base of the burgundy panel. Finish the tag with a double ribbon bow placed between the rose and the heart. Tie the tag with burgundy ribbon.

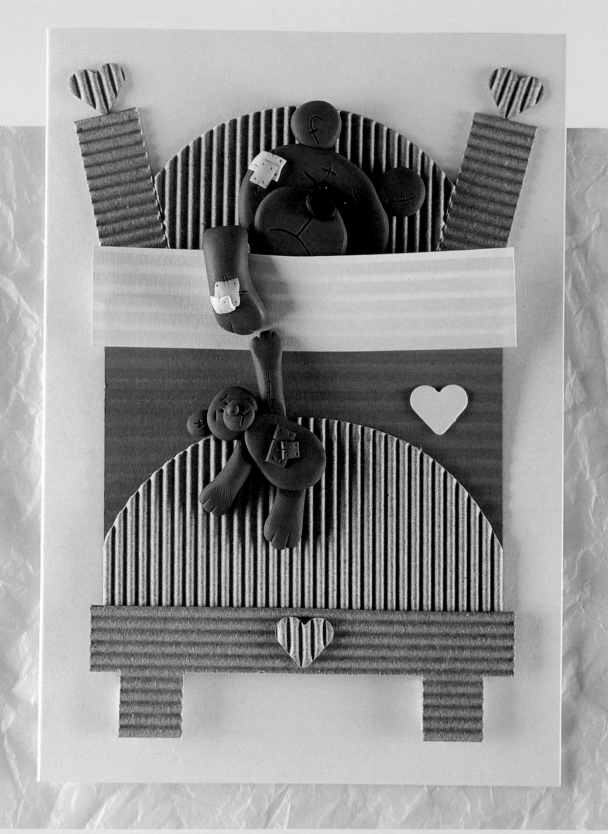

Get well

MATERIALS AND EQUIPMENT

- A6 white card blank
- Corrugated card (buff or natural)
- Bright orange card
- Yellow card
- Small heart craft punch
- Double-sided tape
- Strong PVA glue
- Sticky foam pads
- Two black seed beads
- Pin or sewing needle
- Craft knife
- Pencil
- Ruler
- Tracing paper
- Paper crimper
- Polymer clay (Fimo): caramel, yellow, white, black

Bringing cheer to someone's day is made easy with bright colour. It certainly adds warmth to this bear snuggled up in bed!

Prepare the card

Trace and transfer templates A, B and C (page 116) onto buff corrugated card as follows:

Headboard (A)	Vertically corrugated
Footboard (B)	Vertically corrugated
Baseboard and legs (C)	Horizontally corrugated

Glue or tape the baseboard and legs to the bottom of the footboard. Use a small craft punch to create a vertically corrugated heart. Fix to the centre of the baseboard.

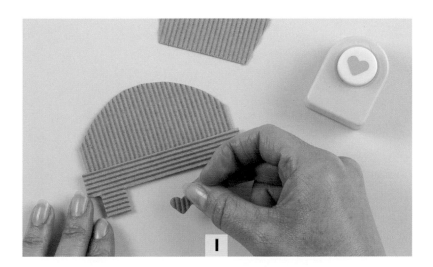

2 For the bedposts, the same colour is used to cut two lengths that are ¹/₂in (13mm) wide x 1⁵/₈in (40mm) deep. The cutting is done on the horizontal for these pieces. Use the punch to create another two vertically corrugated hearts.

3 Measure 2¹/₄in (55mm) from the top of the card and then draw a faint horizontal pencil guideline. Fix the bottom of the headboard on the guide in a central position with glue or double-sided tape. Place and fix the posts in the same way. Glue a heart above each post.

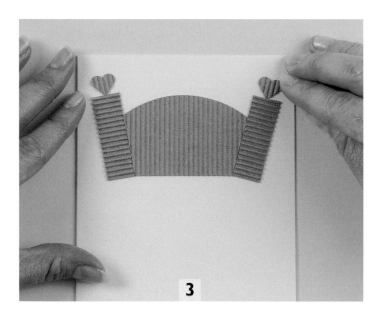

3

4 For the blanket, cut a rectangle that is 3¹/₈in (80mm) wide x 3in (75mm) deep from orange card and a strip of yellow card that measures 3¹/₄in (85mm) wide x ³/₄in (20mm) deep. Trim blanket to suit footboard.

5 Glue or tape the yellow strip to the top of the orange blanket with an overlap of ³/₈in (10mm). Leave to dry if using glue. Pass through a paper crimper to create a broad horizontal textural effect.

6 Secure the footboard with the attached baseboard and legs to the bottom of the blanket. Punch out a small yellow card heart to decorate the blanket.

useful **tip**

● You can either transfer the templates onto white card, making a pattern to cut around, or trace them onto the smooth side of the card.

Bear

7 Using caramel-coloured clay, roll a ball with an ¹¹/₁₆in (17mm) diameter. Work the clay between your thumbs and forefingers, gently flattening to a disc of 1¹/₈in (30mm). Rotate the clay, applying equal pressure all round. Gently stretch to form an oval head.

8 A ³/₈in (10mm) ball, halved, will be sufficient to make two flat teardrops for ears. Press each pointed end into the top of the head.

9 Create the muzzle in the same way as the head using a ³/₈in (10mm) ball of clay. Add a small black nose and score the clay with a pin to create a mouth (you want to achieve a sad look). Press the seed beads into the clay for eyes and then score the eyebrows so that they point downwards.

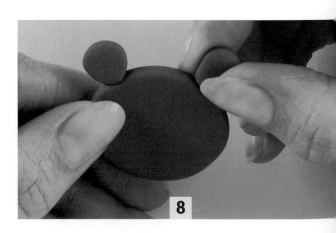

8

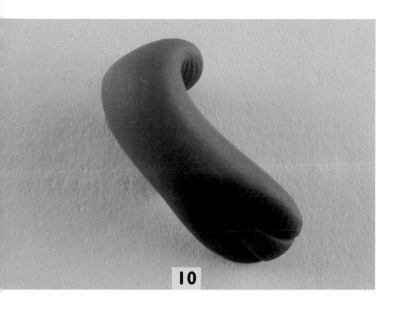

10

Use the same amount for the arm as for the muzzle. Roll into a ³/₄in (20mm) long log. Gently squeeze at one end to create a paw. Use your finger or a sculpting tool to round the edges. Split the paw area by making two cuts into the clay with a craft knife. Make a small inward curve at the top of the arm.

11 Finish the character by adding small clay patches of yellow and lemon (your own mix).

Small teddy bear

12 Form the teddy's body from a ³/₈in (10mm) ball of caramel clay shaped into a flat teardrop. Shape a ³/₁₆in (5mm) ball into a disc for the head then attach it to the body.

13 A small disc is required for the ear and a slightly larger one for the muzzle. Add facial features with a pin and create a tiny nose.

14 Roll another ³/₈in (10mm) ball and divide it into two equal parts for the arms. Shape each piece into a small flat log, adding detail to the paw as described when creating the larger bear.

15 Attach the arms in the position of your choice to the back of the small body. A ⁵/₁₆in (8mm) ball shaped and attached in the same way will provide the teddy's one remaining leg. (It is a much-loved teddy that has seen better days!) Small patches may be added to the body.

Bake

16 Bake all the clay pieces, following the manufacturer's instructions and allow ample time for cooling.

Assemble

17 Use strong, fast-drying glue to set the bear's head at a slight angle on the headboard. On the back of the blanket, apply sticky foam pads to the top corners. Add one to the base of the footboard and another in the middle of the entire area. Support the legs with smaller pieces of sticky pad. Remove the backing strips and attach to the card, covering part of the bear's muzzle. Glue the shaped arm over the top of the blanket. Allow the small teddy bear to dangle just below the bear's paw and use the same glue to hold it in place.

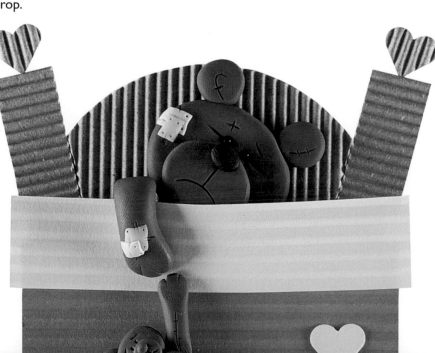

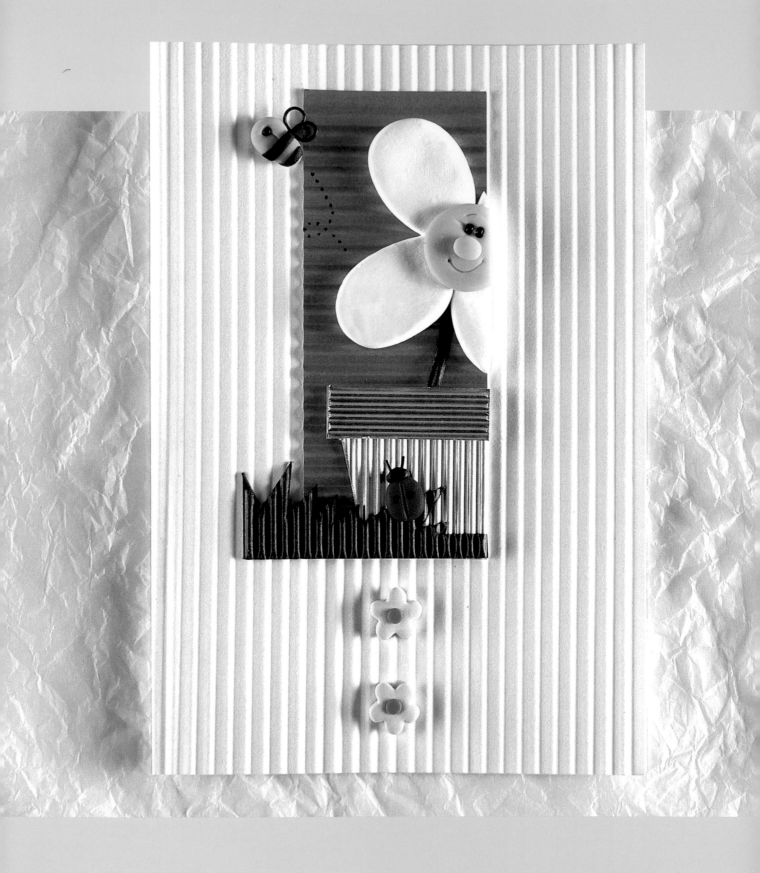

Mother's day

Make it special and say it with flowers on Mother's Day. Create this bright and cheerful card for her enjoyment.

MATERIALS AND EQUIPMENT

- A6 white card blank
- Pearlescent or plain blue card
- Corrugated card in dark green and gold • Ruler
- Craft knife • Paper crimper
- Black seed beads
- Scissors • Tweezers
- Craft wire – black 22-gauge
- Double-sided tape
- Strong PVA glue
- Pin or similar tool
- Clay cutter – 1/2in (13mm) flower
- Polymer clay (Fimo): white, black, yellow, red, peppermint blue

For the matching gift tag:

- Corrugated card in dark green and gold • Cream card
- Green pearlescent card
- Gold lamé ribbon – 1/4in (6mm) width • Natural raffia
- Black craft wire
- Small single-hole punch
- Polymer clay (Fimo): red, black

Prepare the card

1 Open the card and pass the front through a paper crimper. Stop at the fold, leaving the back of the card untouched. Crimping will shorten the card front. Trim the back to suit.

2 Cut a rectangle that is 1 5/8in (40mm) wide x 3 3/4in (95mm) deep from blue card, crimp it then place it towards the centre top of the card, fixing its position with double-sided tape or PVA.

1

3 Trace the flowerpot templates (A and B, page 117) then transfer the images onto gold corrugated card and cut out. Fix the lip of the pot to the main shape with double-sided tape.

4 Form a 2in (50mm) length of grass from green corrugated card, cutting the blades with irregular jagged edges. From the same card, cut a thin stem for the flower.

5 Place the flowerpot, grass and stem aside. These parts are not fixed at this stage.

Small flowers

6 Mix together small amounts of yellow and white clay then use a clay cutter to create two small lemon-coloured flowers. Add a little blue dot of clay to each centre.

Ladybird (ladybug)

7 A ³/₁₆in (5mm) ball of red clay flattened into an oval will provide the body. Use a craft knife to make a clean vertical indent on the body to represent the bug's wing case then add a small black ball to create the head. If you feel confident, make the tiny spots from black clay; otherwise, mark with a permanent pen after baking when the clay is cool.

8 Insert two tiny lengths of black wire into the top of the head to form the bug's antennae.

Bee

9 Use a ³/₁₆in (5mm) ball of yellow clay flattened into an oval for the body. Insert a bead for the eye and create tiny thin black bands of clay for the body stripes. These can also be penned at a later stage, if preferred.

10 Use a small length of black wire to form the wings (see *useful tip* on facing page). Loop the wire at one end (a). Create a loop to the other side (b). Press the wire flat with your fingers and cut to leave a small stem. Insert the wire stem into the top of the bee's body.

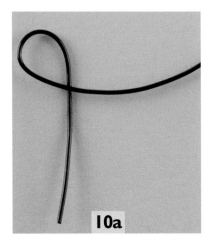

10a

10b

Large flower

11 Start with a ³/₄in (20mm) diameter ball of white clay and divide the quantity into four equal parts. Roll each section into a ball. Now they can be formed into flat discs and gently stretched at one end to make petals. Place together, creating a flower formation.

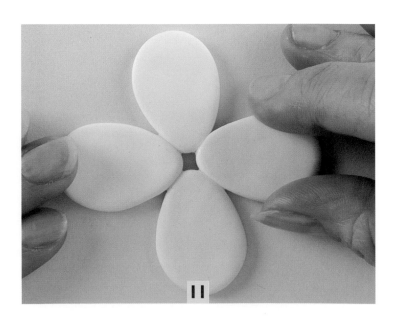

11

1 3 Place the flowerpot at the base of the blue panel on the card. Do not glue into position. Place the unbaked flower above at an angle, with an overlap to the blue panel and white card. Score into the clay with a craft knife to mark the position of the overlapping petal area.

useful tip
● Use a pair of tweezers to control the bending of the wire.

12 A ³/₈in (10mm) ball of yellow clay shaped into a disc will enhance the flower by giving it a centre. Flatten the clay between your thumbs and fingers. Keep the clay turning, applying equal pressure to ensure a perfectly formed circle. Insert beads for the eyes, roll a small ball of yellow for a nose and scratch the mouth and eyebrow detail using a pin. Place on top of the petals.

14 Lift the flower from the card and place it on your work surface. Remove the marked section. Use a metal ruler for a clean, straight edge and cut through the clay with your craft knife.

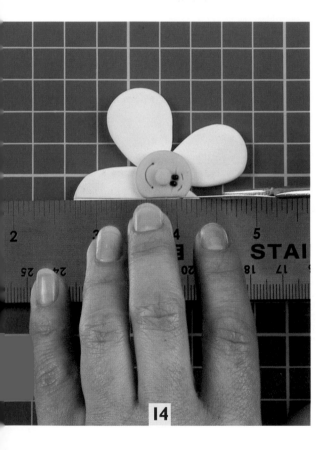

14

Bake

15 Bake all of the clay pieces following the manufacturer's recommendations and allow ample time for cooling.

Assemble

16 Assess the position of the flower to the flowerpot to determine the stem length required and then cut to suit. When satisfied, glue or tape the card parts into position. Finally, fix the characters to the card.

Matching **tag**

1 Create a gold flowerpot shape that is $2^5/8$in (65mm) high, similar to that in the card project. Cut the lip of the pot as a separate piece.

2 Cut a 2in (50mm) high tag shape from cream card. Punch a hole in the top. Thread the tag with raffia and secure it to the top of the pot. Attach the lip.

3 Cut three leaves from pearlescent green card and another from green corrugated card. Group the pale green leaves together with edges overlapping. Hold their position with a little glue. Punch a hole in the top of the grouped leaves and single leaf.

4 Punch a hole in the top left corner of the flowerpot and attach the leaves to the pot with raffia. Thread gold ribbon through the same holes and tie in a bow.

5 Make the ladybird slightly larger than the card project, using the same method. Bake the clay.

6 Glue the little bug in position and add a message to the swing tag.

Thank you

MATERIALS AND EQUIPMENT

- Pearlescent orange card blank
  – 5in (125mm) sq.
- Warm yellow card
- Green card
- Pencil
- Ruler
- Craft knife
- Pin
- Tracing paper
- Strong PVA glue
- Four black seed beads
- Compass cutter
- Polymer clay (Fimo): pastel lemon,
  golden yellow, orange

Bright colours have been incorporated into this design to bring vibrancy to the card. It lends itself to being used for many occasional greetings.

Prepare the card

1 On green card, cut out a rectangle that is approximately 3in (75mm) wide x 4in (100mm) deep (see the template provided on page 117).

2 Use the template to trace the inner image onto yellow card then cut out.

3 Glue the yellow pattern to the green rectangle in a central position and centre both on the card blank.

useful tip
- A compass cutter, if available, is to your advantage when cutting the arc to the top of the pattern. 'X' marks the position of the compass point.

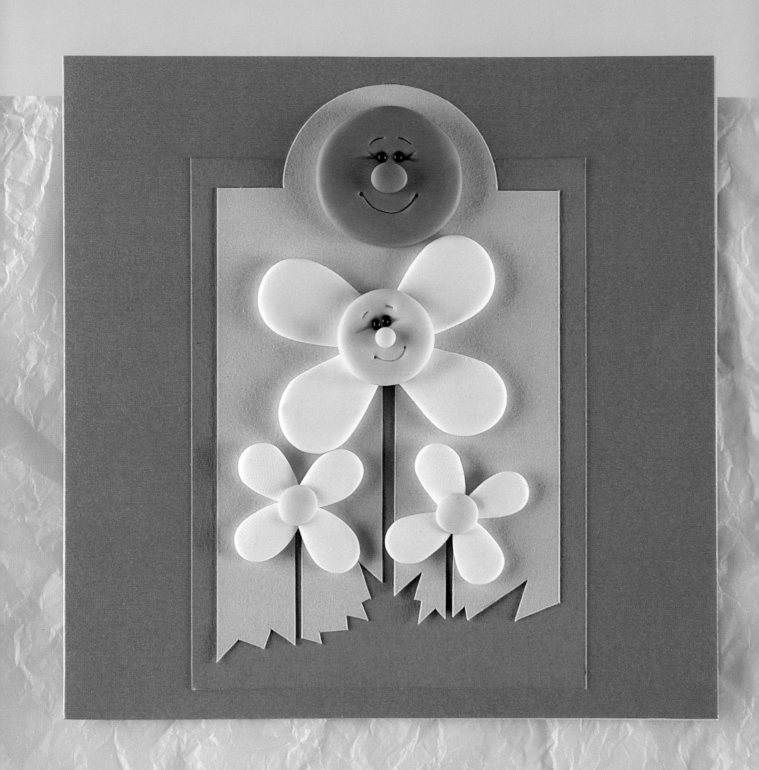

Small daisies

4 The small daisies at the base of the card originate from a ¹/₂in (13mm) ball of pastel lemon clay. Use a craft knife to divide this quantity into eight equal parts. Form simple petal shapes (small teardrops) from each. Position four petals together with points joining at the centre. Repeat to create another daisy.

5 Split a ¹/₄in (6mm) ball of golden yellow clay in half. Re-roll each piece into a ball and form two small discs. Press a disc into the centre top of each daisy.

Large daisy

6 Form the large daisy from an ¹¹/₁₆in (17mm) ball of the petal colour previously used. Only four sections are required. Divide the clay equally and shape each petal as before.

7 A ³/₈in (10mm) ball of golden yellow, shaped into a disc, will provide the daisy with a head. Position the head. Add a small, ball-like nose. Insert two beads as eyes and scratch facial features into the clay with a pin.

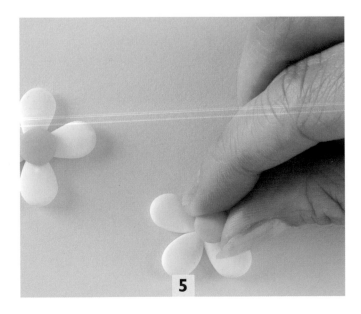

5

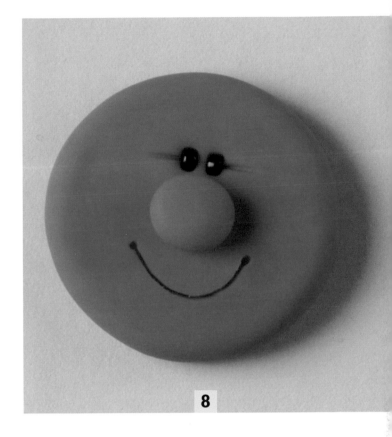

8

Sun

8 Roll a ⁵/₈in (15mm) ball of orange clay and work the clay between your fingers until a disc diameter of approximately 1¹/₈in (30mm) is obtained. Create the sun's face in the same way as for the daisy.

Bake

9 Bake the sun and the daisies, following the manufacturer's instructions. Allow ample time for cooling.

Assemble

10 Carefully remove the clay parts from your baking surface. Place the sun within the yellow arc and arrange the daisies on the stems below. Use strong glue to fix them into position.

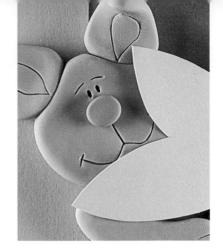

Easter bunny

MATERIALS AND EQUIPMENT

- Lime-green card blank (DL size)
- Bright blue lightweight card
- Yellow lightweight card
- Scallop-edged scissors
- Dark green corrugated card
- Craft knife
- Double-sided tape
- Ruler
- Pencil
- Strong craft glue
- Tracing paper
- Cocktail stick or pin
- Polymer clay (Fimo): sahara,
  red, white

The freshness of spring is captured in the use of bright colours and a simple arrangement of daffodils.

Prepare the card

1 Use a pencil to lightly mark a rectangle that is 1⅝in (40mm) wide x 4⅜in (110mm) deep on the centre front of the card blank. Cut and remove this area to create an aperture.

2 Cover the inside front of the card with a blue card insert. Secure with double-sided tape (see *useful tip* on page 60).

3 Use the same colour of card to cut two rectangles measuring 1⅝in (40mm) x 3½in (90mm). Fix above and below the aperture, placing the top rectangular panel flush with the card edge and the base panel to the fold line.

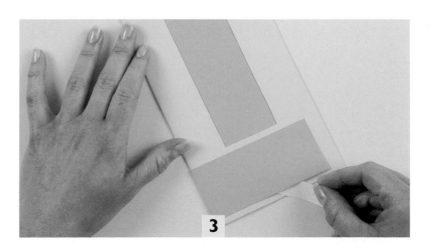

3

Daffodils

4 Trace templates A and B (page 117) and cut two daffodils from yellow card. Trim the tops of both flower trumpets with scallop-edged scissors then pass each trumpet through a paper crimper. Alternatively, use corrugated card.

5 Cut two narrow lengths measuring 3¹/₈in (80mm) from green corrugated card to create the stems.

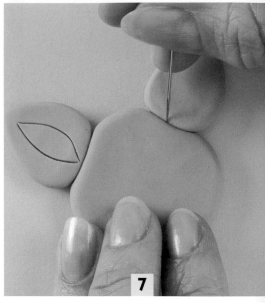

8 Simply mix a small amount of red clay to white to form a pink nose. Facial features can then be scored using the same method as applied to the inner ears.

9 Roll a sahara-coloured log shape from a ⁵/₈in (15mm) ball to an approximate length of 1³/₈in (35mm). Bend and gently flatten to form an arm. Round the corners at each end and use your craft knife to make two cuts into the paw area.

Rabbit

6 Create the rabbit's head from a sahara-coloured clay ball with a diameter of ³/₄in (20mm), flattened between the thumbs and forefingers to form a disc that has a diameter of 1³/₈in (35mm).

7 Model the ears from another ball measuring ¹¹/₁₆in (17mm), divided into two equal parts. Shape each into a 1in (25mm) long teardrop. Firmly press each ear into the top of the head. Score the inner ear detail with a pin. Bend the tip of one ear.

useful tip

● When securing card with double-sided tape, release small pieces of the backing paper, folding them back to form little tabs. Position and hold the card in place. Gently pull on the tabs to fix its position.

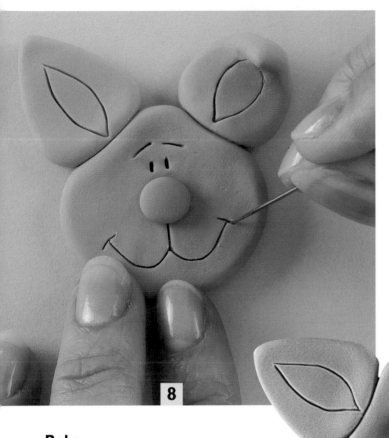

8

Bake

10 Bake the two clay pieces at the recommended temperature and allow time for cooling.

Assemble

11 Use glue or double-sided tape to fix the trumpet of each flower to the petal area, then a small piece of tape to fix a stem to the back of each flower. Glue one assembled daffodil towards the top of the card at an angle. Cut away the excess stem.

12 When fixing the other flower in position, apply glue or tape to all parts, excluding the petals to the left of the daffodil. Cut away any excess to the outer edges of the card.

13 Allow any glued card pieces to dry. Carefully lift the unglued petals and secure the rabbit's head to the card. Fix the arm into position, gripping the stem.

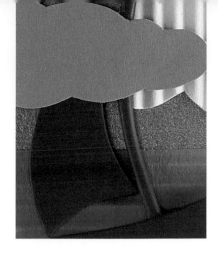

Father's day

MATERIALS AND EQUIPMENT

- A6 silver pearlescent card blank
- White card
- Bright blue card
- Dark blue card
- Double-sided tape
- Tracing paper
- Pencil
- Ruler
- Craft knife
- Pin or sewing needle
- Sticky foam pads
- Non-stick roller
- Paper crimper
- Strong glue
- Polymer clay (Fimo): red

Forget the traditional sepia tones often used for this occasion and focus on something more modern. Create a crisp look with cool colours.

Prepare the card

1 Trace cloud templates A and B (page 118) onto white card. Use a craft knife or scissors to cut out the shapes and then pass the clouds through a paper crimper.

2 On bright blue card, draw a rectangle that is 1³/₄in (45mm) deep x 2¹/₄in (55mm) wide. Cut out the shape and crimp the card as before.

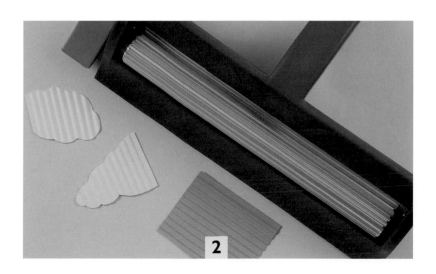

3 Use double-sided tape to secure the rectangle in a central position, 1in (25mm) from the base of the card.

4 Apply double-sided tape to each white cloud. Fix the smaller cloud ³/₈in (10mm) from the top left of the card with a side margin that is equal to that of the base rectangle. Now secure the other white cloud to the right-hand side in precisely the same way.

5 Trace cloud template C and wave template D (page 118) onto bright blue card and repeat the wave pattern on a darker blue card. Now cut out the shapes. These pieces will be used in the final assembly of the card.

Yacht

6 Trace the yacht templates (E and F, page 118) onto a piece of paper. Use a non-stick roller to roll out red clay to a depth of approximately ¹/₁₆in (2mm). Ensure you have enough clay to accommodate the templates. Refer to *Tips and techniques*, *Tracing onto clay*, pages 20–21. Cut around the traced shapes with a craft knife.

7 Create the mast by rolling a small amount of red clay into a 2¹/₄in (55mm) long thin log. Finish the top of the mast with a small clay ball of the same colour. Gently flatten the base of the mast and attach the hull. Bend the mast slightly to create a gentle curve.

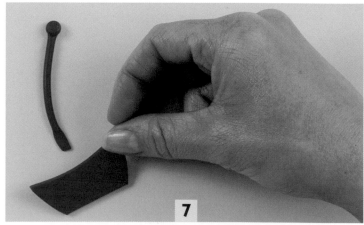

Bake

8 Keep the sail separate from the hull and mast when baking. Bake the clay according to the printed instructions on the product packaging and allow time for cooling.

Assemble

9 Carefully remove the yacht and sail from your baking surface. Place the yacht onto the blue card base at an angle and secure with strong glue. Use the same adhesive to secure the sail to the left side of the mast.

10 Attach sticky pads onto the back of the bright blue cloud. Fix into position, leaving a ³/₈in (10mm) margin to the left of the card. The depth added by using sticky pads gives the impression of the cloud passing in front of the yacht.

11 To complete the card, fix sticky pads to the back of the wave patterns prepared earlier. Fix the darker wave to the baseline of the crimped rectangle. Offset the remaining wave, leaving the side and base margins as before.

Best wishes

MATERIALS AND EQUIPMENT

- Pearlescent white card blank
  – 5in (125mm) sq.
- Black card • Pieces of scrap card
- Circular cookie cutter – 1³/₈in
  (35mm) diameter
- Small star cutter
- Non-stick roller
- Craft wire – silver 22-gauge
- Scissors • Double-sided tape
- Craft knife • Strong PVA glue
- Cocktail stick or pin
- Polymer clay (Fimo): peppermint
  blue, apple green, white

For the matching gift tag:

- Silver card and black card
- White pearlescent paper
- Silver craft wire
- Small circular cookie cutter
- Small single-hole punch
- Clay cutter – ¹/₂in (13mm) star
- Polymer clay (Fimo): peppermint
  blue, white

Up, up and away! The cleverly placed black background panel dramatically enhances the swirling colours of these balloons and the use of silver wire ties the whole project together.

Prepare the card

Cut out a black rectangle that measures 2in (50mm) wide x 3¹/₂in (90mm) deep. Attach double-sided tape to one side and peel off the backing. Fix at the top of the card, leaving equal margins on either side.

Balloons and stars

2 Use one part white clay to two parts blue – ³/₈in (10mm) diameter ball of white mixed with a ³/₄in (20mm) ball of blue – and likewise white to green. Rolling and twisting the two colours together will achieve a marbled effect (refer to *Tips and techniques, Marbling*, on page 19).

3 When the technique has been applied, roll each marbled colour to a depth of ¹/₁₆in (2mm). Use a small cookie cutter to cut a disc from each.

4 Cut a small triangle of each colour. Fix the triangular pieces at the base of each marbled disc to form the tied area of balloon.

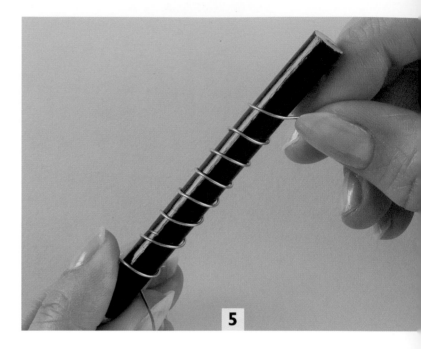

5 Cut a length of silver wire that is 9³/₄in (250mm) long. Wrap the wire around a pencil to create a loose spiral. Slide the wire from the pencil and stretch to loosen further. Cut into two equal lengths.

6 Place both wires on a piece of card then place another piece of card on top. Use a roller to flatten the wire between the two sheets of card and feed the flattened wire into the back of each balloon. Try to avoid piercing the front; the wire should sit just below the surface of the clay.

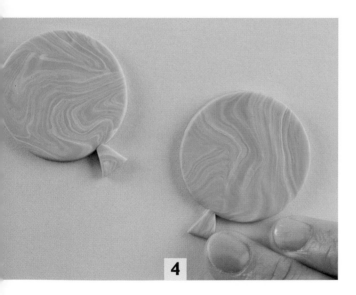

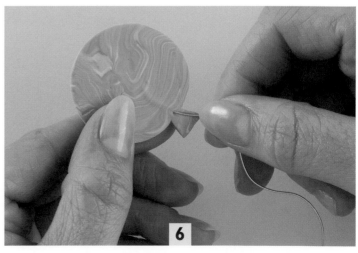

7 Repeat the marbling technique, using a smaller quantity of clay. Use a cutter to create two green and three blue stars. Place a blue star on the green balloon and a green star on the blue balloon. The other three stars will be used when assembling the card.

8 Mix a very small amount of each marbled colour with a little white clay. Mix the clay thoroughly and roll it until thin. Create highlights for each balloon by cutting small, curved rectangles. Lift the thin highlights with your craft knife blade and fix their position.

9 Any remaining marbled blue clay can be worked further into a solid colour. You will need a 3/8in (10mm) diameter ball in order to create a bow. Remove a small ball from the mix to form the bow's knot. Cut the remaining quantity in half and form two teardrops. Arrange the teardrops with points joining and place the ball on top. Extra detail in the form of creases or folds can be added to the bow by using a pin or cocktail stick to make small indentations into the clay's surface.

Bake

10 Bake all the clay parts according to the manufacturer's recommendation. The wire inserted into each balloon remains attached during the baking process. Allow time for cooling.

Assemble

11 Arrange the balloons on the card and secure with glue. Attach the bow on top of the wire strands below the black background panel. Cut away the excess wire at the base of the card. Set the remaining stars at random on the card and secure with glue.

Matching tag

1 Cut a piece of silver card measuring 4in (100mm) wide x 3 1/2 (90mm) deep then fold the card in half. Cover the bottom half of the tag with white pearlescent paper.

2 Fix black card measuring 1 1/8in (30mm) wide x 4 1/2in (115mm) deep to the top in a central position. The strip will overhang the tag length.

3 Punch a small hole in the top left corner of the tag front. Feed a length of wire through the hole and then twist to secure. Curl the ends as desired.

4 Create the wire-strung balloon in the same way as for the card project. Use a cutter to remove a star shape from the balloon and then use the removed piece as part of your design. Bake the clay and adhere the balloon and star to the tag.

Happy birthday

MATERIALS AND EQUIPMENT

- Pearlescent blue card blank
  – 5in (125mm) sq.
- Golden yellow card
- Green card
- Double-sided tape
- Strong glue
- General scissors
- Decorative craft scissors
- Craft wire – black 22-gauge
- Black seed beads
- Pin
- Pencil
- Ruler
- Tracing paper
- Craft knife
- Non-stick roller
- Mini number cookie cutters
  (optional)
- Polymer clay (Fimo): apple green,
  orange, pacific blue, red, black

This hungry caterpillar is specially designed with the younger generation in mind, although its cheeky features are bound to appeal to the child in all of us.

Prepare the card

I Cut a panel that is approximately 4in (100mm) wide x 3½in (90mm) deep from golden yellow card and centre it on the card blank, using double-sided tape to fix the position. Open the card and cut away the top right corner with decorative scissors.

2 Trace the leaf template on page 118 and transfer it onto green card. Cut the shape and use decorative scissors to create 'caterpillar damage' to the outer edges. Fix the leaf onto the card with glue or double-sided tape.

Caterpillar

3 Prepare apple green clay balls with the following diameters:

1 ball – $9/16$in (14mm)
2 balls – $7/16$in (11mm)
2 balls – $3/8$in (10mm)
1 ball – $6/16$in (9mm)
1 ball – $5/16$in (8mm)
1 ball – $6/16$in (9mm)

Lay the balls out on your work surface in this order. Shape the largest ball of clay into a disc of approximately 1in (25mm) to form the head. Create a teardrop from the last ball prepared and shape all the others into ovals by starting with a disc and gently stretching the clay outwards.

4 With your finger, flatten a small area at the top of each oval. This will allow you to place one segment on top of the other without creating too much bulk when assembling the segmented body. Once all the segments have been joined, carefully bend the body to suit.

5

5 Add a small, ball-like nose to the centre of the head and insert two beads above as eyes. Create a small disc for the cheek and use a pin to scratch the mouth and eyebrow detail. The added detail suggests the caterpillar's mouth is rather full.

6 Decorate the seven segments with small balls of orange clay, placed to the right side of the body. Use the same quantities of green clay to add sucker-like feet to segments 2–6.

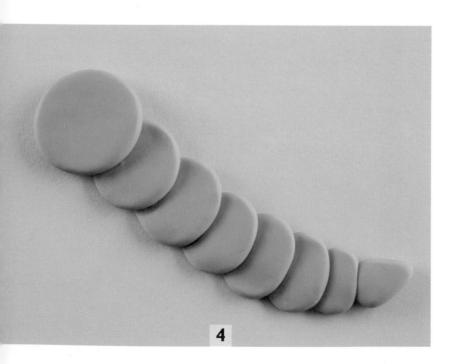

4

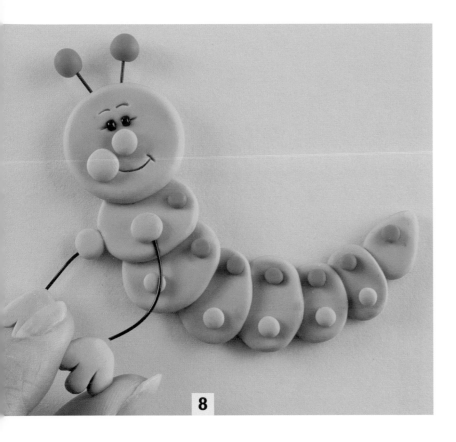

8

10 Place the number beneath the caterpillar's hands. Apply gentle pressure to hold it in place.

Ladybirds (ladybugs)

11 Roll three $^3/_{16}$in (5mm) balls of red clay then flatten each into a small disc. Make a vertical indent in each body with the craft knife blade. Add a small black head to each and insert tiny cuts of wire as antennae. The ladybird spots can be added either in the form of black clay or penned in with a black permanent pen after baking.

Bake and assemble

12 Position one ladybird on top of the caterpillar's body. Bake all the pieces at the recommended temperature. Allow the clay to cool thoroughly then glue the characters onto the card.

7 Cut three lengths of black wire, each measuring 1in (25mm). Snip one of them in half and insert these pieces into the top of the caterpillar's head. Add small balls of orange clay to decorate the tops of the antennae. Gently curve the other two pieces of wire to create the arms, inserting one into the outer edge of the first segment and the other lying across the first and second segment. Hold each arm in position by covering the wire ends with small discs of green clay. Make these slightly larger than the sucker-like feet.

8 Form two little green hands from a $^3/_8$in (10mm) ball of clay, halved and shaped into rounded triangles. Make two cuts into the widest end of each to create fingers. Open the fingers and round the edges. Press the hands onto the exposed wires.

9 A single number can be placed between the caterpillar's hands, if you wish. Use small number cutters for the age being celebrated. Cut the numeral of your choice from pacific blue clay, rolled to a thickness of $^1/_{16}$in (2mm).

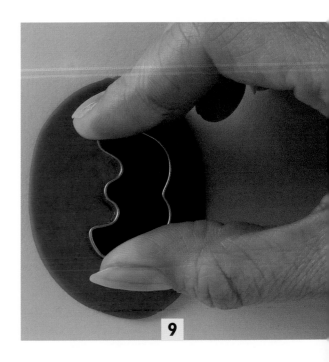

9

Anniversary

MATERIALS AND EQUIPMENT

- A6 silver card blank
- White card
- Silver card
- Red paper
- Cookie cutter – 1³/₈in
  (35mm) heart
- Clay cutter – ¹/₂in (13mm) heart
- Small heart craft punch
- Small single-hole punch
- Seed beads
- Non-stick roller
- Sewing needle or pin
- Pencil
- Ruler
- Craft knife
- Eraser
- Decorative scissors
- Strong PVA
- Sticky foam pads
- Polymer clay (Fimo): mother
  of pearl, silver

This card is designed to be appropriate for any celebratory year. The emphasis on the colours used, though, makes it perfect for a silver wedding anniversary.

Prepare the card

1 Position the card in landscape format. Measure and lightly mark a horizontal pencil guide, ⁵/₈in (15mm) from the card base. Mark the centre of this guide. Use a craft punch to punch a heart into either side of the centre point, leaving a gap of 1¹/₈in (30mm) between the shapes.

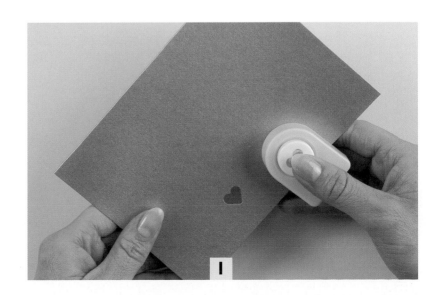

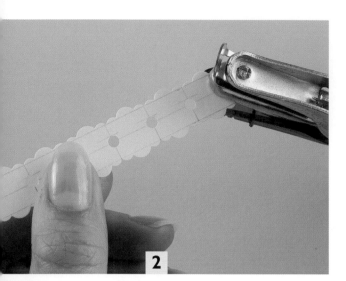

2 On white card, mark out a rectangle that is 4in (100mm) deep x ³⁄₈in (10mm) wide. Cut along the outside of the marked length with decorative scissors to create a double-edged frilly strip, ensuring a match to the pattern on either side. Mark a central line through the length of the frilled strip. You may wish to mark this line at equal intervals as a guide for punching. Punch out small holes with a hand-held punch to create a simple lace effect. Repeat this process to form another lace strip. The first strip can be used as a template to avoid further measuring.

3 Position the lace at the top left side of the card and trim to fall in line with the punched hearts. Erase all the pencilled guides. Fix the position with PVA glue. Repeat for the opposite side.

4 Choose a good-quality red paper (90–100g) to make a folded insert. Make the insert slightly smaller than the card. Secure to the inside back of the card with double-sided tape or glue, placed below the fold.

5 Trace and transfer the heart template (A, page 119) onto silver card and cut out. Use a craft punch to prepare a white card heart. Place these pieces aside to be used later.

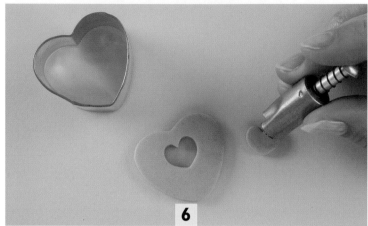

The loving couple

6 Add a little silver to pearl clay. Make sure the colours are well mixed together and that you have enough to accommodate the heart-shaped cookie cutter. Roll the clay to a depth of ¹⁄₈in (3mm) and cut the shape. Place the small heart clay cutter just above the centre of the silver heart and punch out the shape. Do not discard the removed area – it will be used in the final assembly. (If you do not have a heart-shaped cookie cutter, see *useful tips* below.)

useful tips

• If a small heart cookie cutter is not available, use template B on page 119. See Tips and techniques, pages 20–21 for Tracing onto clay.

• Change the colours to suit the anniversary being celebrated. Consider using red or pink as the predominant colour in this design to send a loving wish on Valentine's Day.

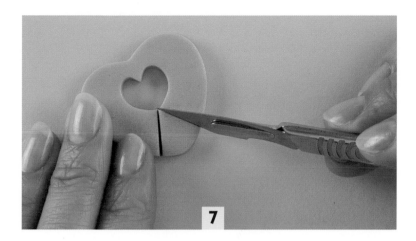

7 From the base of the cut-out, use a knife to cut left and right diagonals through the clay to the outer edges of the silver heart. Remove this piece and, on removal, two little arms will be formed.

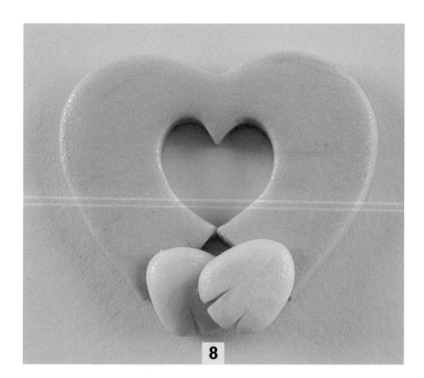

8 Form small pearl-coloured hands from a 3/8in (10mm) ball of clay split into two equal parts. Mould each into little rounded triangles then use a knife to cut into the clay to form fingers. Overlap the hands, joining them together, and then attach to the ends of the arms.

9 From pearl clay, form a ball that has a 5/8in (15mm) diameter. Split it into two equal parts then re-roll each into a ball. Create the characters' heads by gently squeezing and flattening each into discs that are approximately 1/8in (3mm) thick. Make and attach two small noses of the same colour and insert beads as eyes. Use a needle or pin to scratch out the facial features.

10 Make a little bow (model two very small teardrops with a tiny ball on top) from the mixed silver clay (prepared earlier) and attach at an angle on the decided female head.

Bake

11 Place all the modelled pieces (heads unattached) on a suitable baking surface. Bake as recommended by the manufacturer and allow the clay to cool thoroughly.

Assemble

12 Glue the heart-shaped arms and the two heads to the silver card heart prepared earlier. Apply sticky foam pads to the reverse of the card shape. Centre on the card, just above the fold. Glue the small silver clay heart between the punched shapes to the base of the card then apply adhesive to the white card heart and position above.

Pampered pooch

MATERIALS AND EQUIPMENT

- White pearlescent card blank
  – 5in (125mm) sq.
- Green card
- Forest-green card
- Pencil
- Ruler
- Eraser
- Craft knife
- Needle or pin
- Small heart craft punch
- Clay cutter – 1/2in (13mm) flower
- Double-sided tape
- Strong PVA glue
- Polymer clay (Fimo): white, red,
  caramel, silver

Create a delightful card that can be used for lots of occasions. This content puppy is sure to be admired by everyone.

Prepare the card

1 Cut a simple kennel shape from green card (see template on page 119) then cut an inner panel of forest-green card that measures 2in (50mm) wide x 1 3/8in (35mm) deep for the entrance. Fix the card pieces together and secure at the top of the card blank in a central position. Use a punch to create a decorative heart from forest-green card and glue above the kennel entrance.

Puppy

2 Flatten an 11/16in (17mm) ball of white clay into a disc with a 1 1/8in (30mm) diameter, then stretch the clay at one end to form an egg-shaped head that is 1 5/8in (40mm) in height.

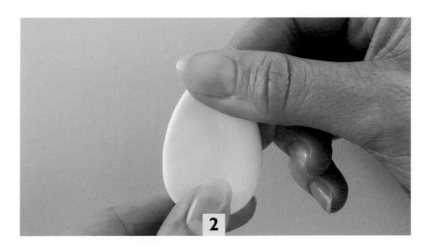

3 Use the same colour for the muzzle. You will require a ³/₈in (10mm) ball shaped into an oval. Place the muzzle at the base of the head. Insert beads above as eyes. Mark the mouth and eyebrow detail with a pin.

4 Create the ears from a ¹/₂in (13mm) ball of white clay. Roll the clay into a log that is 1⁵/₈in (40mm) long and halve it with a knife. Flatten each piece between your fingers and fold the clay over at one end to create floppy ears. Attach the ears to the underside of the head.

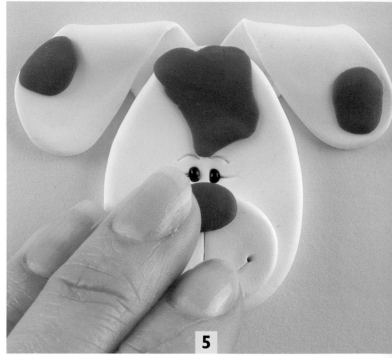

5

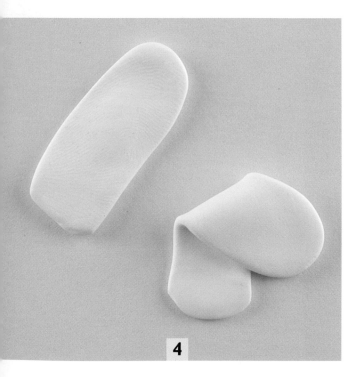

4

5 Squeeze small amounts of caramel clay between your fingers to create very thin irregular-shaped patches and randomly place them on the puppy. Shape and place a small oval nose of the same colour.

6 Prepare a ³/₈in (10mm) ball of red clay and roll into a log that measures 1¹/₈in (30mm) in length. Gently flatten and wrap around the base of the puppy's head to make a collar. Add little silver clay studs on top.

Bowl of bones

7 Start with a ⁵⁄₈in (15mm) ball of white clay. On a flat surface, roll the clay into a log that is 4¹⁄₈in (105mm) in length. Use a knife to split the length into five parts. Round off all the cut edges.

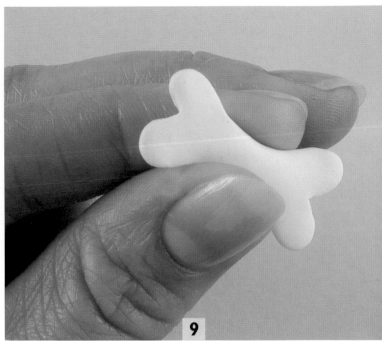

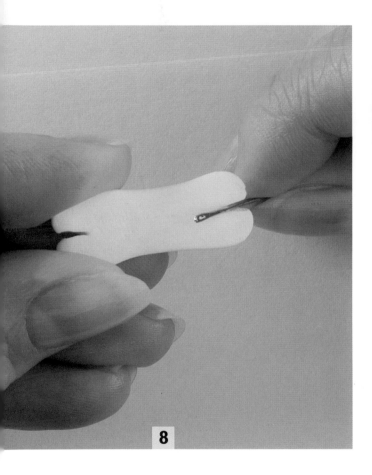

8 Press each piece with your finger to flatten and then press the side of a needle or pin into the flattened logs to open the ends. Shape and round the edges of each indent.

9 Gently squeeze the middle of each shape to complete the modelling of the bones. Cross-stack the bones, keeping the assembled stack as flat as possible.

10 Shape a ⁵⁄₈in (15mm) ball of red clay into a cube. Continue to press and stretch the clay into a lozenge shape. Add a gentle curve to the shape to create the bowl. Fix the bones with an overlap at the top of the bowl.

Flowers

11 Prepare small, flat amounts of white and red clay and use a clay cutter to create a flower in each colour. Use the same colours to add contrasting flower centres.

Bake

12 Bake the clay according to the manufacturer's recommendation and allow time for cooling.

Assemble

13 To complete your card, use a strong PVA glue to carefully adhere each of the clay pieces to the card.

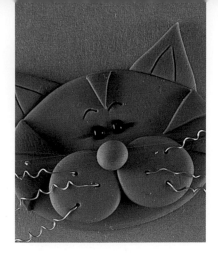

Feline antics

This is a really fun card that is sure to be adored by all cat lovers!

MATERIALS AND EQUIPMENT

- Pearlescent orange card blank
  – 5in (125mm) sq.
- Terracotta card
- Gold card
- Pencil
- Ruler
- Craft knife
- Sewing needle or pin
- Black seed beads
- Household fuse wire (5 amp)
- Double-sided tape
- Sticky foam pads
- Strong glue
- Polymer clay (Fimo): cognac,
  caramel, white

Prepare the card

1 On terracotta card, measure and cut out a rectangle that is 4¹/₂in (115mm) wide x 3³/₄in (95mm) deep. Use double-sided tape to secure it to the top of the card in a central position.

2 Prepare two gold squares measuring 2in (50mm) to be used later in the design.

Cat

3 Work a ⁵/₈in (15mm) diameter ball of cognac clay into a disc and stretch it into an oval of 1³/₈in (35mm) for the head.

4 Use your fingers to flatten a small quantity of the same colour and cut two triangular-shaped ears. Attach them to the head.

5 For cheeks, use a ³/₈in (10mm) ball of clay split into two equal parts and shaped into discs. Position at the base of the head.

6 Place a small nose on top. Insert the beads above the cheek area as eyes. Use a needle or pin to mark eyebrows and detail to the inner ears and cheeks.

7 Flatten a little caramel clay and cut out small triangular pieces to form the markings on the cat's face. Position the shaped pieces at the outer edges of the head and cut away any excess.

7

8 Cut six small lengths of fuse wire to create whiskers. Wrap a section of each loosely around a sewing needle. Slide the wire from the needle and insert the whiskers into the cheeks.

Skeletal fish

9 Form the fish heads from a 3/8in (10mm) ball of white clay. Split the quantity in half and shape two rounded triangles that are approximately 5/8in (15mm) long.

10 Use the same amount of clay, shaped as before, to form the tails. Remove a triangular section from each base.

11 Roll a 5/16in (8mm) ball of white clay into a log that is 31/8in (80mm) long. Cut in half with a craft knife. Attach the fish heads and tails to each thin log and build on the skeleton by placing small horizontal logs of the same thickness on top.

12 Bend each skeleton into a curve. Eye detail can be added by making a little hole with a needle or pin.

Paw prints

13 Divide a 5/8in (15mm) ball of caramel clay into four parts. Shape each into a rounded triangle. Use your finger to indent each base. Smooth the edges to form heart-shaped pads. Flatten a 3/8in (10mm) ball of the same colour and cut sixteen equal sections. Re-roll each into a ball and arrange four to the outer edges of each pad. Press gently to secure.

Bake

14 Bake the clay pieces at 265°F/130°C for 30 minutes if using Fimo. Follow the manufacturer's instructions if using a different brand of clay. Allow to cool.

Assemble

15 Glue the cat's head and a fish skeleton to the gold card squares prepared earlier. Apply sticky foam pads to the reverse and position to the left of the card, leaving equal margins at the top and bottom. Glue the remaining pieces in the position of your choice.

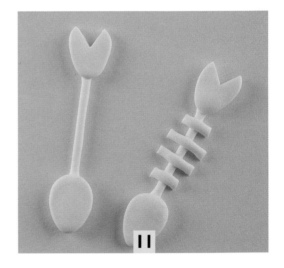

11

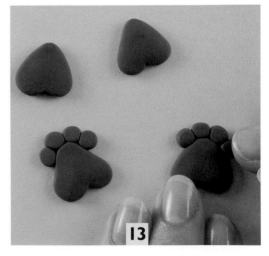

13

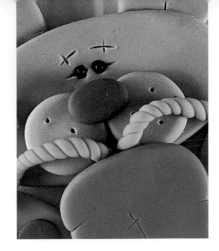

Carrot patch

MATERIALS AND EQUIPMENT

- Pearlescent orange card blank
  – 5in (125mm) sq.
- Lime-green card
- Yellow card
- Paper crimper
- Ruler
- Pencil
- Craft knife
- Pin
- Black seed beads
- Double-sided tape
- Strong PVA glue
- Polymer clay (Fimo): sahara,
  caramel, orange, apple green

Animal antics always capture the heart. This card is suitable for many occasions and animal lovers alike.

Prepare the card

1 Cut a yellow card rectangle that measures 4¹/₂in (115mm) deep x 3¹/₂in (90mm) wide. Pass through a crimper. Corrugated card may be used for the same effect. Affix double-sided tape to the rectangle and attach to the fold on the card blank.

2 Tear a rectangular piece of lime-green card and fix at an angle to the centre of the card in the same way. Use PVA if preferred.

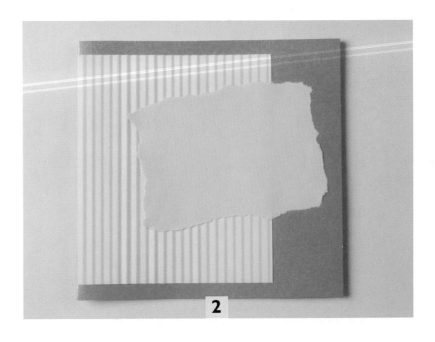

Rabbit

3 Prepare four sahara clay balls, each with a diameter of $5/8$in (15mm). Start by flattening three balls into discs measuring $1^1/8$in (30mm) wide and stretch each into a shallow oval of $1^3/4$in (45mm). These ovals will form the rabbit's head and feet.

4 Select two ovals to be used as feet. Stretch these further at one end to make tapered drops that are approximately $2^1/4$in (55mm) in length. Shape the pieces with your fingers until similar shapes are obtained. On a flat surface, make two cuts into the widest part of each foot with a craft knife.

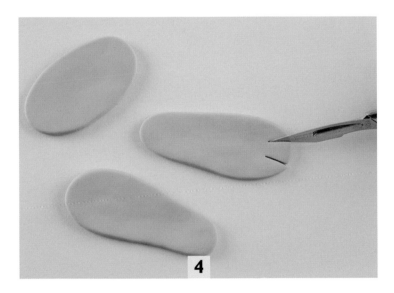

4

5 Use the remaining clay ball to form the floppy ears. Split the clay in half. Re-roll each piece into a ball then shape into flat teardrops that are approximately $1^1/8$in (30mm) long. Stretch and fold the tapered ends. Flatten the base of each ear and fix to the underside of the head.

6 Form the cheeks from a $3/8$in (10mm) ball of the same colour. Halve it and create two small discs and position them at the base of the head. Position a caramel-coloured oval nose to the centre top of the cheeks. Use a pin to make small holes in the cheeks to represent the presence of whiskers. Insert two beads above as eyes. Eyebrows can also be marked with a pin.

7 Prepare a $3/8$in (10mm) ball of caramel clay. Split evenly and create two flat, stretched, teardrop-shaped pads. Fix in position at the base of the feet. Form the small pads from a $3/8$in (10mm) ball of the same colour, divided into six equal parts. Shape into small balls. Arrange them around the large pads on the feet. Press the balls flat with your finger to secure. Position the feet at an angle below the rabbit's head.

Carrot

8 Create the carrot from a $5/8$in (15mm) ball of orange clay. Shape into a flat, rounded triangle, long enough to cover the area from the base of the feet to the cheeks. Make small indents into the sides of the carrot with a craft knife. Do not attach at this stage.

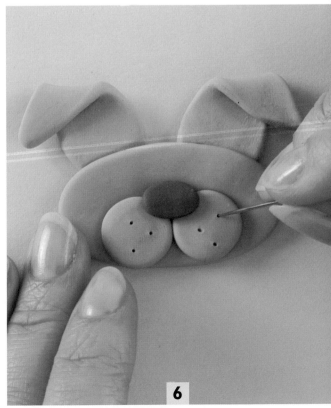

6

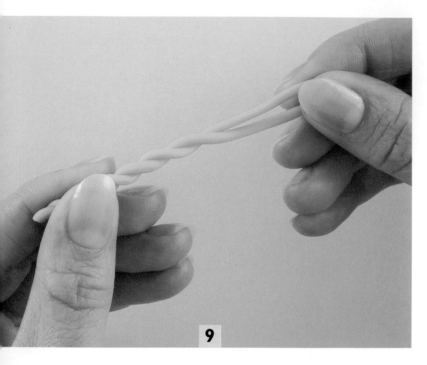

9

11 Fix the twisted carrot top to the underside of the carrot. Position the carrot between the rabbit's feet and then press the carrot gently at the top and bottom to secure.

12 Bend the green twists, allowing them to fall onto each foot. Gently press to secure. The character should now be well held together. Use the colours of your choice to add little patches to the rabbit and mark small stitches with a pin.

Bake

13 Bake the modelled rabbit according to the instructions and allow to cool.

Assemble

14 Carefully remove the cooled piece from your chosen baking surface and fix to the card with strong, fast-setting PVA glue.

10

9 Create the carrot top from a long length of green clay, rolled thin. Fold the length in half and twist the strands of clay together.

10 Pinch the centre of the twisted log and cut the lengths on either side to suit.

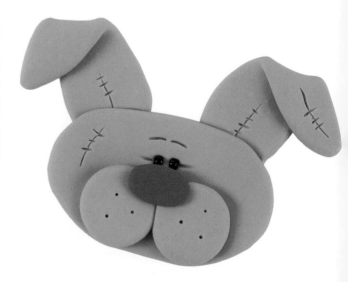

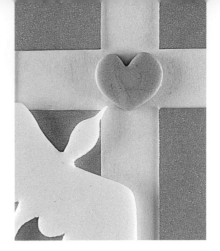

Wedded bliss

MATERIALS AND EQUIPMENT

- Pearlescent white card blank – 5in (125mm) sq.
- Silver coloured paper
- White ribbon – ¹/₈in (3mm) width
- Small single-hole punch
- Plain and decorative scissors
- Ruler
- Pencil
- Double-sided tape
- Strong craft glue
- Non-stick roller
- Tracing paper
- Paper
- Pin
- Clay cutters – ¹/₂in (13mm) flower and heart
- Polymer clay (Fimo): pearl, silver

Design a simple but effective card that will be a pleasure to receive, using pearls and metallic combined with delicate white ribbon.

Prepare the card

Open the card blank and use a single-hole punch to punch out two holes in each side on the card front, leaving a generous space between each. Thread a piece of white ribbon through the punched holes and then fix the ribbon ends to the inside front with a little craft glue.

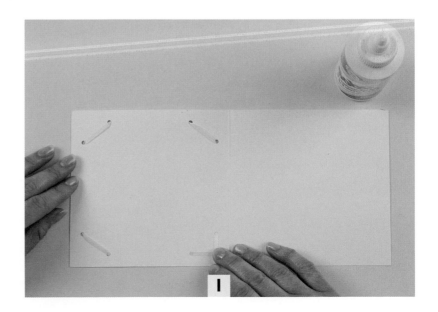

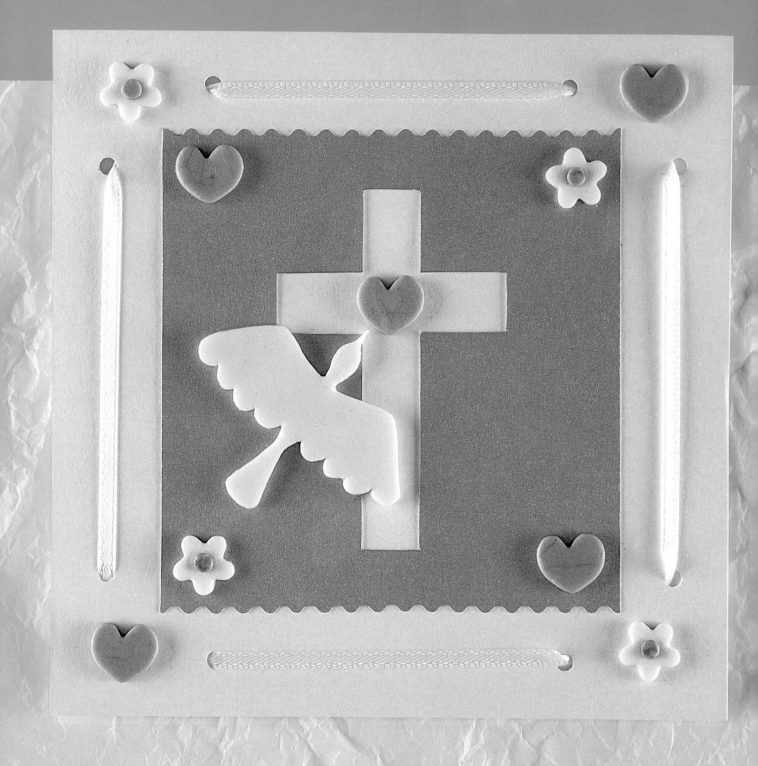

2

Bake

5 Bake all the clay pieces, following the manufacturer's recommendation. Remove your work from the oven and allow it to cool.

Assemble

6 Use strong, fast-setting glue to secure all the modelled parts to the card. Place a pearl flower in the top left corner of the card followed by a silver heart placed to the right, and continue by reversing that arrangement to the base. Arrange the clay parts in the inner panel, starting with a silver heart to the top left, and so on. Centre the last heart within the cross and set the dove at an angle.

2 Measure a 3³/₈in (85mm) square onto silver coloured paper and trim the top and bottom with decorative scissors. From the centre of the square, cut out a cross that measures 2⁵/₈in (65mm) long with a crossbar of 1⁵/₈in (40mm). Fix double-sided tape to the reverse of the silver panel and set in a central position on the card.

Hearts, flowers and dove

3 Roll small amounts of pearl and silver clay to a depth of approximately ¹/₁₆in (2mm). Use clay cutters to create four pearl flowers and five silver hearts. Decorate each flower centre with little balls of silver clay.

4 Transfer the dove template on page 119 onto white paper and trace around the pattern with a pin onto pearl-coloured clay, rolled to a maximum depth of ¹/₁₆in (2mm). Use your craft knife to cut this shape.

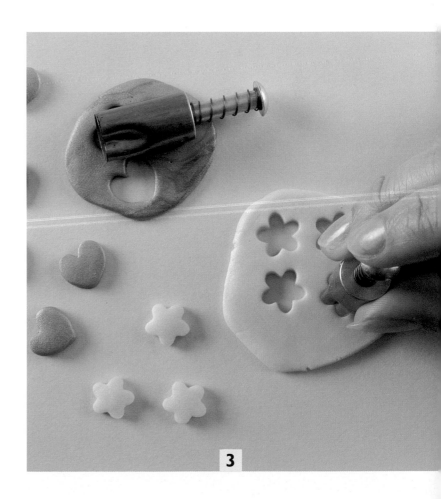

3

Bridal buds

MATERIALS AND EQUIPMENT

- A6 cream card blank
- Lilac paper
- Cream corrugated card
- Cream card
- Cream ribbon – $1/8$in (3mm) width
- Small heart craft punch
- Double-sided tape
- Strong PVA glue
- Pin or sewing needle
- Ruler
- Pencil
- Eraser
- Craft knife
- Scissors
- Polymer clay (Fimo): apple
  green, white

Create this beautiful card with hearts and flowers in soft cream and white – perfect for a special couple on a day to remember.

Prepare the card

1 From lilac paper, cut out a panel that is $2^3/8$in (60mm) wide to cover the length of the card. Apply double-sided tape to the lilac paper then peel off the backing strips and centre on the cream card blank.

2 On cream corrugated card, measure and cut out a rectangle that is $3^1/4$in (85mm) wide x $1^3/8$in (35mm) deep. Align the corrugated piece to the left of the lilac panel. Fix in position with double-sided tape, $1^1/8$in (30mm) from the top of the card. Cut away any excess at the card edge.

3 Punch out three hearts from plain cream card using a craft punch. Glue on a heart, $3/8$in (10mm) from the centre top and bottom of the card. Fix the final heart $1^5/8$in (40mm) from the base of the card.

Bow

4 Cut approximately 8in (200mm) of ribbon. Gently fold the ribbon in half to determine its centre then pin the centre of the ribbon onto a piece of scrap paper.

5 Start to create the bow. Work close to the pin, marking your centre.

6 When complete, carefully remove the pin, holding it in place. Further tightening of the bow will be required. Cut the ribbon ends to the desired length. Glue the bow to the card, below the cream corrugated strip.

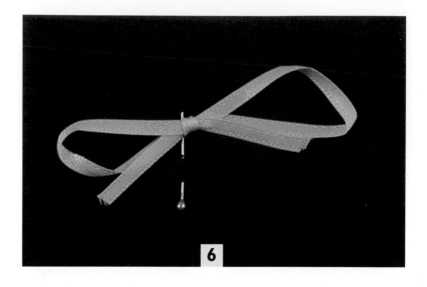

Rose buds

7 Condition enough white clay to form a ball with a 3/4in (20mm) diameter. Roll out on a flat surface into a log measuring 53/4in (145mm) then use a knife to cut it into twelve equal parts.

8 Squeeze each section between your fingers to thin the clay. Gently roll each piece inward to form a small coil. Pinch and roll the bottom of each shaped bud into a small stem. (Refer to the photographs featured in the *Be mine* project, pages 42–45.)

9 On your work surface, place four buds side by side, with another four placed on top.

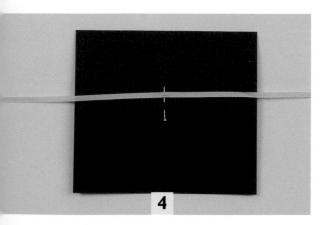

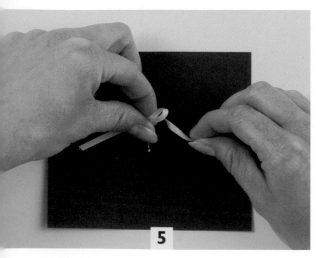

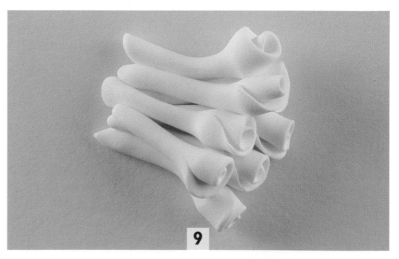

10 Carefully lift the buds and randomly place the remaining four, leaving small gaps for greenery. Now, gently press all the stems together.

11 Use a knife to remove the bulk of the clay gathered at the base of the arrangement to achieve flat-backed buds.

Leaves

12 Create small apple-green teardrop-shaped leaves to fill the gaps. Use your own judgement with regard to the quantity and size.

13 Bend to suit and vein the leaves with a pin if desired.

14 Attach the leaves to the base of the buds. Ensure the base area remains flat for gluing in the final stage.

Bake

15 Bake the rose bud arrangement on a suitable baking surface, following the clay manufacturer's recommendation. Allow time to cool before lifting the piece from the baking surface.

Assemble

16 Glue the floral arrangement onto the cream corrugated card.

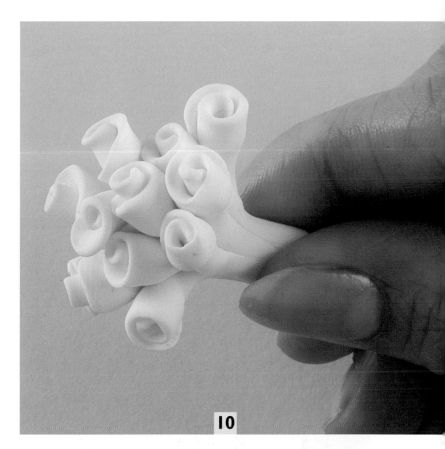

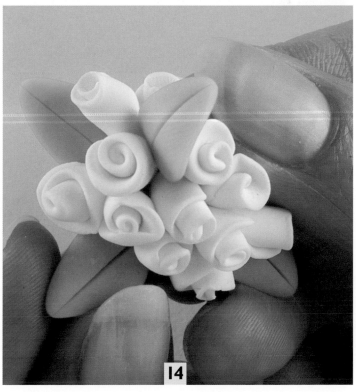

Trick or treat

MATERIALS AND EQUIPMENT

- Pearlescent orange card blank
  – 5in (125mm) sq.

- Golden yellow card

- Black card

- Tracing paper

- White paper

- Pencil

- Ruler

- Craft knife

- Pin

- Black permanent pen

- Decorative craft scissors

- Non-stick roller

- Sticky foam pads

- Strong glue

- Double-sided tape

- Computer and printer

- Polymer clay (Fimo): orange,
  leaf green

Send a card to celebrate Hallowe'en

or create a party invitation!

Prepare the card

1 With decorative scissors, cut out rectangles of black card measuring approximately 4in (100mm) wide x 3^{1}/$_4$in (85mm) deep and 1^{5}/$_8$in (40mm) wide x 1^{3}/$_8$in (35mm) deep.

2 Using the same scissors, prepare a yellow rectangle that is approximately 4in (100mm) wide x 3^{1}/$_2$in (90mm) deep. Apply double-sided tape to the reverse and fix to the large black rectangle in an offset position. Use the tape to secure both to the top left side of the card.

3 Use a craft knife to cut out a black rectangle that is 2^{3}/$_4$in (70mm) wide x 2^{5}/$_8$in (65mm) deep and then position it within the fancy-edged panels.

4 Refer to template C (page 120) and use the pattern to create two bats out of black card.

Pumpkins and tendrils

5 Roll and condition a 1in (25mm) ball of orange clay. Use a non-stick roller or a clay-dedicated pasta machine to roll the clay out to a thickness of 1/16in (2mm).

6 Refer to templates A and B (page 120) and trace the pumpkins onto white paper. Transfer the tracings onto the clay. (See *Tips and techniques, Tracing onto clay*, pages 20–21.) Use a knife to cut the face from the large pumpkin.

7 Overlap the two small pumpkins. Flatten a very small amount of leaf-green clay and provide each pumpkin with a small triangular-shaped stock.

8 Roll two thin logs of the same colour into approximately 5 1/8in (130mm) lengths and make random curls and twists in the clay to create two creeping tendrils.

7

6

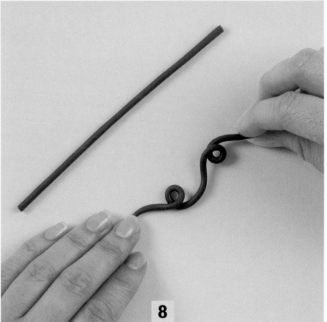

8

Bake

9 Bake the pumpkins and tendrils at the time and temperature recommended then allow to cool.

Assemble

10 Apply glue to the back of both tendrils and place at the base and right side of the prepared card. Fix sticky pads to the small black decorative rectangle cut earlier and position at the bottom right corner.

11 Use a black permanent pen to add detail to each pumpkin. Allow the ink to dry before sticking them to the card, as smudging may occur.

12 Finally, add very small pieces of sticky pads to the wings of each bat and allow them to take flight in the position of your choice.

Design reproduction (for invitations)

The card design needs only to be created once. It can then be colour copied at your local photocopying shop. Some shops will supply you with (if asked) the image repeated on one sheet of paper. Reduced reproductions of the design are a sure way of cost-cutting. Your design time is also dramatically reduced as the designs can now be cut and pasted onto a plain white card. Create a computer-generated insert on paper to transform the card design into a party invitation. Refer to the example shown. The size of the insert will be governed by the card blanks being used as invitations. A strip of double-sided tape placed at the top of each insert will hold the position within each card.

Invitation

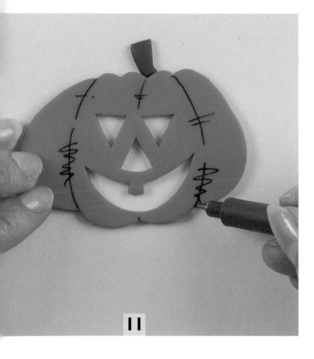

11

useful **tip**

● Any accidental ink smears can be removed by gently scraping the surface of the clay with the blade of your knife. (Avoid using the point of the blade.)

Hallowe'en is Coming

You are invited to:

....

....

On ....

At ....

Time ....

R.S.V.P.   *Fancy Dress*

Star of wonder

MATERIALS AND EQUIPMENT

- DL-sized pale blue card blank
- Bright blue card
- Silver card
- Silver snowflake table confetti
- Silver-edged organza ribbon
  - 1¹/₂in (38mm) width
- Strong PVA glue
- Double-sided sticky pads
- Double-sided tape
- Craft knife
- Pencil
- Cookie cutters (two star designs)
  - approx. 2¹/₂in (63mm)
- Templates provided as alternative
- Polymer clay (Fimo): mother of
  pearl, silver

This attractive Christmas card will be appreciated by people of all ages.

Prepare the card

1 Cut two rectangles measuring 3¹/₄in (85mm) x 7³/₄in (195mm) from bright blue card. Fix double-sided tape to one rectangle and secure to the card front in a central position. Place the other piece of card aside.

2 Cut a length of ribbon, making sure that you have included the card length and an extra ⁵/₈in (15mm) at the top and bottom.

3 Apply small beads of glue along one edge of the ribbon and then fix to the centre of the card, holding the ribbon taught until the glue adheres.

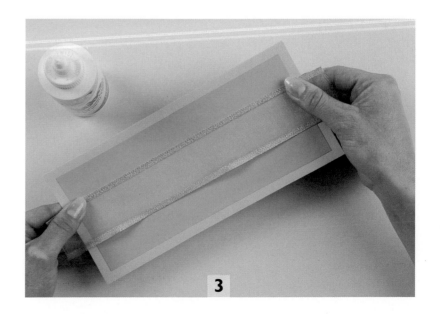

3

4 From silver card, cut out two rectangles that are 2in (50mm) wide x 2³/₈in (60mm) deep.

5 Using a pencil, lightly mark a 1¹/₈in (30mm) margin to the top and bottom of the card and to the outer edges of the ribbon. These guides mark the position of each silver rectangle.

6 Lift the ribbon then glue snowflake confetti above the marked guide at the top of the card and below the guide to the base.

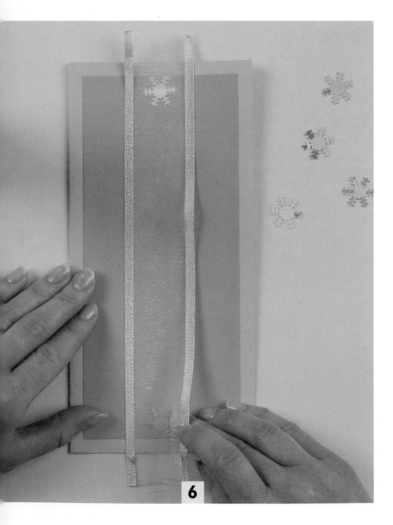

7 Secure the remaining edge of the ribbon to the card with small beads of glue along the edge, as before. The extra ribbon at the top and bottom can be folded over and secured to the inner front with small strips of double-sided tape placed along the raw edge.

8 Apply double-sided tape to the remaining blue rectangle cut earlier. Fix to the centre inner front of the card, covering the ribbon ends.

9 Place sticky foam pads at the back of each silver rectangle to create depth. Centre each rectangle on top of the ribbon at the guides marked.

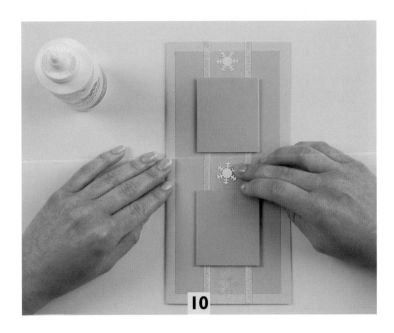

10 Glue a piece of snowflake confetti onto the ribbon between the silver panels.

Stars

11 You will require a quarter block of pearl clay and the same quantity of silver. Condition the clay and roll each colour to a depth of $^1/_{16}$in (2mm). Use cookie cutters to create a pearl-coloured eight-point star and a pearl shooting star. Repeat the cuts on silver clay. Place the silver shooting star on top of the pearl star of the same design. Offset slightly. Offset the eight-point stars in the same way.

Bake

12 Carefully lift the stars onto a baking surface of your choice. Bake the clay according to the manufacturer's recommendation. Allow time for cooling.

Assemble

13 Fix the modelled stars to the silver panels on the card with strong adhesive.

useful tips

• If cutters are not available, refer to templates A and B on page 120. Trace the templates and refer to *Tips and techniques, Tracing onto clay,* pages 20–21.

• Cutters usually provide you with a cleanly cut shape, but any ragged edges can be smoothed with your finger.

Christmas baubles

MATERIALS AND EQUIPMENT

- A6 white card blank
- Purple card
- Pencil
- Ruler
- Craft knife
- Scissors
- Double-sided tape
- Strong glue
- Circular cookie cutter – 1³/8in (35mm) diameter.
- Craft wire – silver 22-gauge
- White ribbon – ¹/8in (3mm) width
- 3D fabric paint – pearl silver
- Polymer clay (Fimo): mother of pearl, lavender, silver

For the matching gift tag:

- Silver card
- Purple card
- White ribbon – ¹/8in (3mm) width
- Clay cutter – ¹/2in (13mm) star
- Small circular cookie cutter
- Polymer clay (Fimo): lavender, silver

Modern colours and simple shapes adorn this festive greeting card, making it a striking and contemporary gift.

Prepare the card

1 Measure ³/4in (20mm) from the top of the white card and cut an aperture of 1³/4in (45mm) wide x 2⁵/8in (65mm) deep. Speckle the card front with very small dots of fabric paint to create a simple representation of snow (see *useful tips* on page 107). Place the card aside. Lie it flat and allow plenty of drying time.

2 Cut a purple card insert, slightly smaller than the card front, to be used in the final assembly of the card.

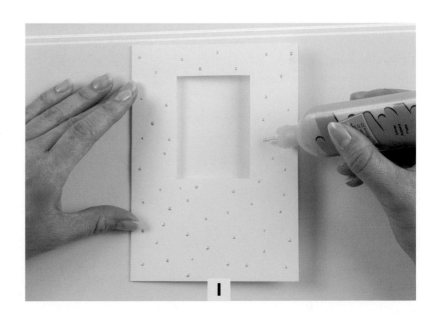

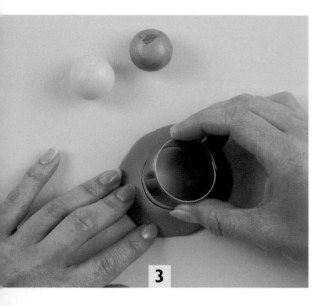

3

Baubles

3 Roll out 1in (25mm) balls of pearl, lavender and silver clay to a depth of 1/16in (2mm). Use a circular cutter on each colour to create three baubles.

4 Create the bauble tops from small, flat blocks of each colour, placed at the top of each bauble.

5 Form the highlights on the baubles by simply adding a little pearl clay to lavender and likewise a little silver to pearl clay. Roll the clay as flat as possible and cut out small arcs from the newly mixed colours. Carefully lift these delicate pieces with a craft knife and position them on the baubles. The silver bauble is not highlighted.

6 Now cut a 2³/8in (60mm) length of silver wire for the baubles' loops. Use scissors to cut the wire into three pieces. Bend each piece into a small loop and carefully insert them into the bauble tops.

7 Affix the pearl bauble with an overlap to the top of the silver bauble.

Bake

8 Bake the clay pieces, following the manufacturer's recommended instructions.

Assemble

9 Ensure the wire loops are secured with a little glue – they shouldn't be removable. Feed the following lengths of ribbon through each bauble loop: two that are 3¹/8in (80mm) and one that is approximately 8in (200mm). Use the 8in (200mm) length with the lavender bauble. After threading the ribbons, knot each to secure. Apply glue to the back of each knot to ensure their hold.

10 Position the baubles on the card. Secure the ribbon ends to the top inside front of the card with small pieces of tape. Cut away any excess ribbon.

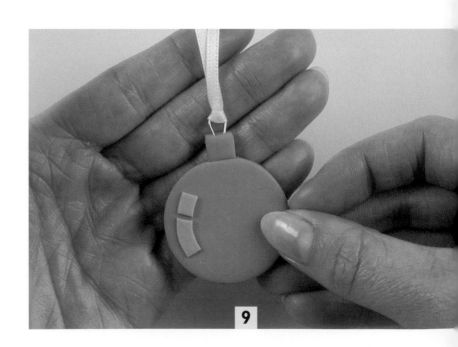

9

11 Apply double-sided tape to the purple insert prepared earlier then fix it to the inner front of the card. Strong glue can now be added to the back of the baubles to hold their position on the card.

12 Create three small white ribbon bows and fix to the top of each bauble loop with a little adhesive of the same kind.

12

useful tips

• Practise on some spare paper before applying the paint to your card blank.

• Three-dimensional fabric paint is available in tubes that are moulded with a fine nozzle for easy application.

Matching tag

1 Cut a piece of silver card that measures 2in (50mm) wide x 3¹/₈in (80mm) deep. Fix a 1¹/₈in (30mm) x 3¹/₈in (80mm) strip of purple card to the left of the silver tag.

2 Add a message to the back of the tag before embellishing it.

3 Create the looped bauble in the same way as for the card project.

4 Roll some silver clay into a thin sheet and cut out a 1in (25mm) x ⁵/₈in (15mm) rectangle. Use a cutter to remove a star shape from the centre. Use the removed shape to decorate the bauble. Bake the clay.

5 Glue the cooled clay pieces in position. Attach white ribbon to the bauble loop.

Stars and stripes

MATERIALS AND EQUIPMENT

- A6 white card blank
- Bright red card
- Dark blue card
- Pencil
- Ruler
- Craft knife
- Tweezers
- Non-stick roller or clay-dedicated pasta machine
- Strong glue
- Double-sided tape
- Clay cutter – ¹/₂in (13mm) star
- Polymer clay (Fimo): white

For the matching gift tag:

- Luggage tag
- White elastic tag tie
- Standard stationery punch
- Dark blue card
- Red card
- Clay cutter – ¹/₂in (13mm) star
- Polymer clay (Fimo): white

Celebrate Independence Day by sending a stylish representation of a most significant American emblem.

Prepare the card

1 On red card, measure and cut out a rectangular panel that is 3¹/₂in (90mm) wide x 5¹/₈in (130mm) deep. Fix strips of double-sided tape to one side. Peel away the backing paper and place it on the card in a central position.

2 Prepare a blue card panel that measures 2in (50mm) wide x 4in (100mm) deep. Fix it to the centre top of the card using double-sided tape to secure.

Stars

3 Use a non-stick roller or a clay-dedicated pasta machine to prepare sheets of white clay. The clay should be approximately 1/16in (2mm) thick.

4 Cut several stars from the prepared sheets, using a cutter to do so. You will require between 27 and 30 stars.

5 Group a few stars together and overlap them to form little stacks. Gently press them together to ensure their hold. Use your own judgement as to how many stacked pieces are required – you will need to create enough to form a mass at the card's base.

Bake

6 Carefully lift and place the stars onto a baking surface of your choice. Bake the clay as recommended by the manufacturer. Allow ample cooling time.

Assemble

7 Lay the stars down the centre of your card, placing the stacked stars to the base. Take time to arrange them in position – try to create a cascading effect. When satisfied with your design, use a pair of tweezers to lift each star to be glued. Fix the small clay pieces to the card.

4

Matching tag

1 Use a luggage tag as a template to cut a tag from white card. Cover the top half of the tag with a rectangular piece of dark blue card. Trim the corners to suit. Use PVA glue or double-sided tape to fix it in position then punch a hole in the centre top.

2 Assemble three strips of red card at equal intervals along the tag base. Leave a small gap between the strips and the solid colour at the top.

3 Add a message to the back of the tag before fixing the clay embellishments.

4 Create the stars in the same way as for the card project and bake as directed. Glue the stars at random on the tag. Thread the tag with white elastic.

Stars and stripes (2)

This is an alternative project to celebrate Independence Day, using stylized elements that focus on the banner's stripes.

MATERIALS AND EQUIPMENT

- Bright blue card blank
  – approx. 5^{1}/$_4$in (135mm) sq.
- Dark blue card
- Red mulberry paper
- White mulberry paper
- Ruler
- Pencil
- Craft knife
- Scrap card
- Non-stick roller
- Double-sided tape
- Strong PVA glue
- Tracing paper
- Sewing needle or pin
- Clay cutter – ^{1}/$_2$in (13mm) star
- Cookie cutter – 2^{1}/$_2$in (63mm)
  shooting star (template provided
  as alternative)
- Polymer clay (Fimo): metallic
  white, red, pacific blue

Prepare the card

1 Simply tear a rectangular piece of white mulberry paper, approximately 3^{1}/$_8$in (80mm) deep to fit the centre of the card blank.

2 Measure and cut out a 2in (50mm) square from blue card. Position the blue square in the left corner of the torn paper with a 1in (25mm) overlap at the top. Fix the square in place with a little double-sided tape.

useful tip
- When tearing mulberry paper, tear the paper towards you. Tearing in this way will give a rough edge with visible fibres. You may prefer a softer look, though. This is achievable by marking out the required area with a wet paintbrush then tearing along the moistened outline.

3

4

3 Create the red stripes from torn lengths of mulberry paper. The small stripe should fall in line with the base of the blue card square and the larger stripe taking the full width of the white background. Apply beads of PVA to the stripes. Use a small piece of folded scrap card to spread the glue evenly over the surface. Set the stripes in position.

4 Apply small beads of glue to the reverse of the entire piece and position on the card.

Stars

5 Follow these instructions as an alternative to using a cookie cutter. The template on page 120 can be used as a guide for colour layering if a cutter is not available. Trace the template onto a piece of white paper.

6 Mix a little pacific blue to metallic white clay. Roll the mixed colour to a maximum depth of 1/16in (2mm). Refer to *Tips and techniques, Tracing onto clay,* pages 20–21, to form the base shape.

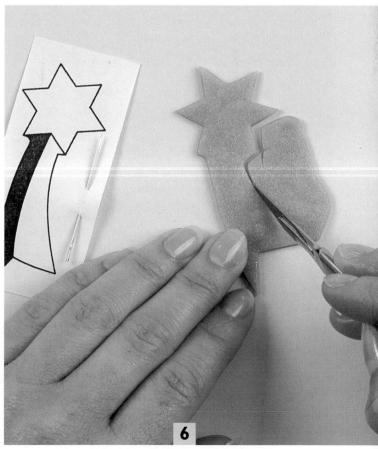

6

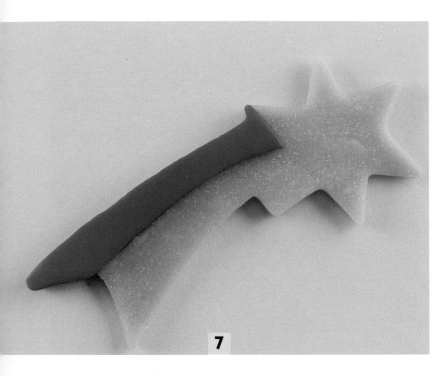

7

8 Prepare metallic white clay for the star at the top of the pattern. Repeat the 'tracing onto clay' technique or use a knife to remove the star if creating the shape with a cookie cutter. Lift from your work surface and carefully set in position.

9 Use a cutter to create four stars from a small sheet of rolled metallic white clay.

Bake

10 Bake the clay according to the manufacturer's recommendation. Allow time for cooling.

Assemble

11 Use PVA to secure the shooting star at an angle on the blue square. Glue the small stars at random onto the card.

7 Roll enough red clay to accommodate the solid area marked on the template. Trace onto the clay as before and cut out. Simply remove the appropriate red section with a knife if preparing the shape with a cookie cutter. Carefully place this piece on top of the blue base.

useful **tip**
● After working with dark-coloured clay, you may have colour deposits left on your hands. Wash your hands before working with the white clay.

Templates

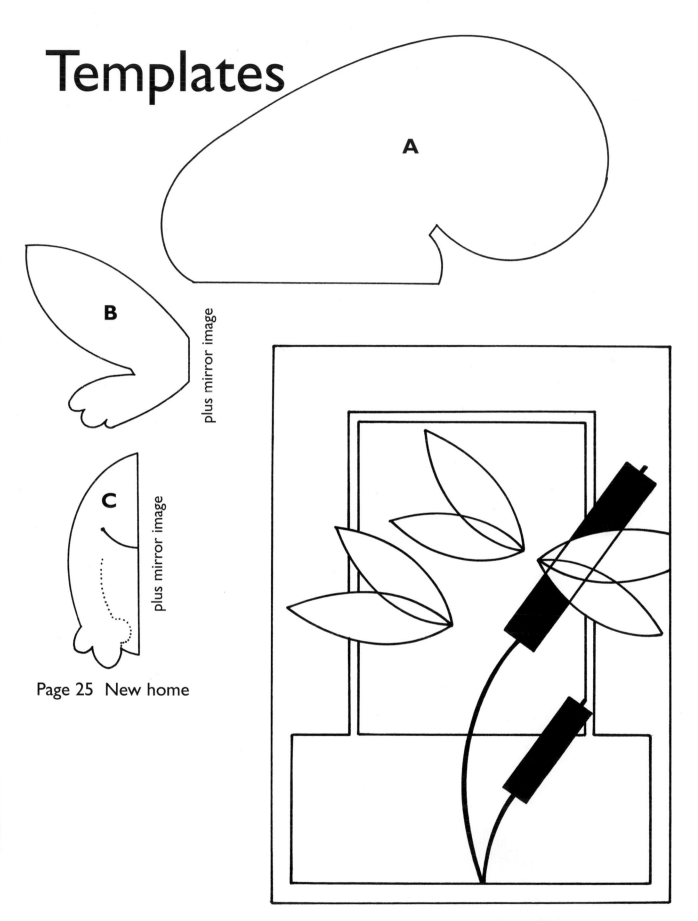

A

B

plus mirror image

C

plus mirror image

Page 25 New home

Page 29 Darting dwellers

Page 31   Heart of gold

Page 35   New arrival

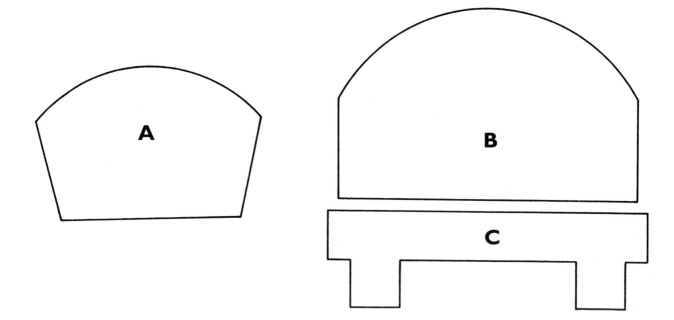

Page 47   Get well

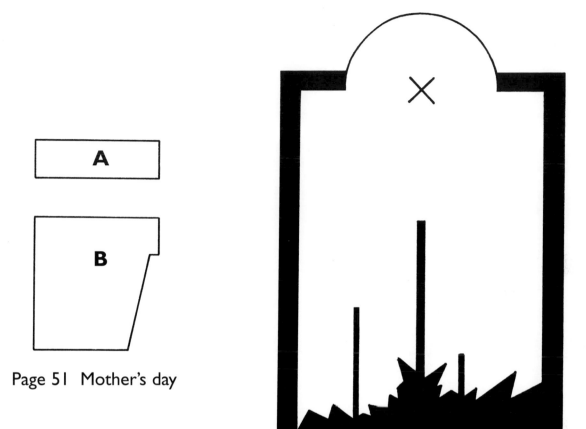

Page 51 Mother's day

Page 55 Thank you

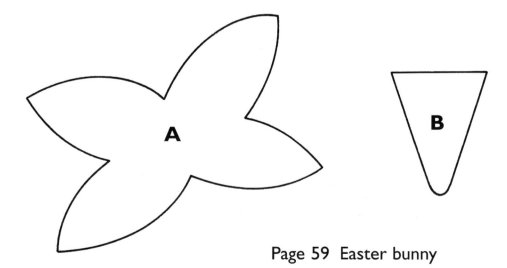

Page 59 Easter bunny

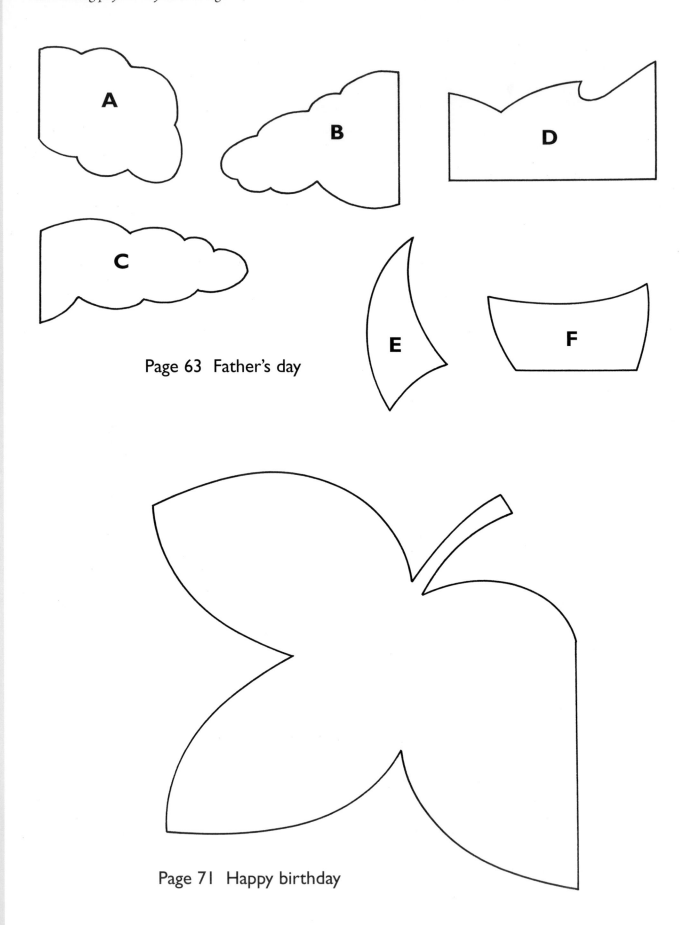

A

B

D

C

E

F

Page 63 Father's day

Page 71 Happy birthday

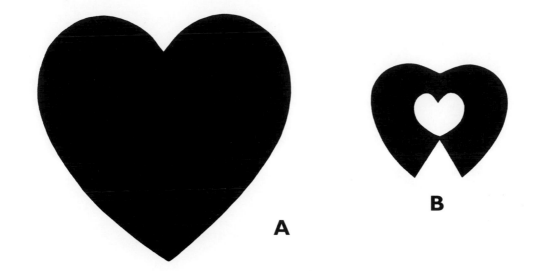

A

B

Page 75 Anniversary

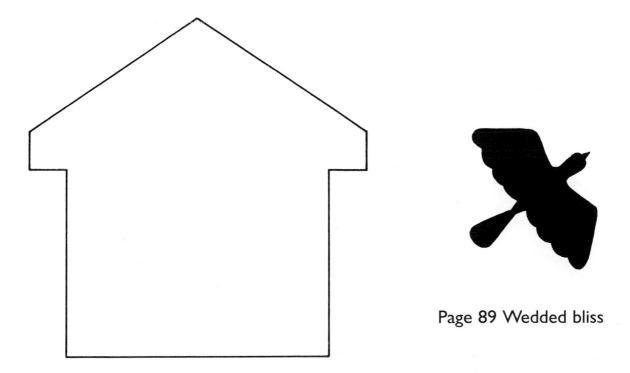

Page 89 Wedded bliss

Page 79 Pampered pooch

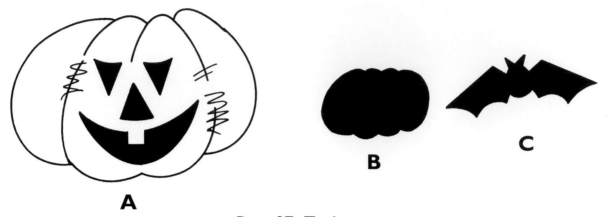

Page 97 Trick or treat

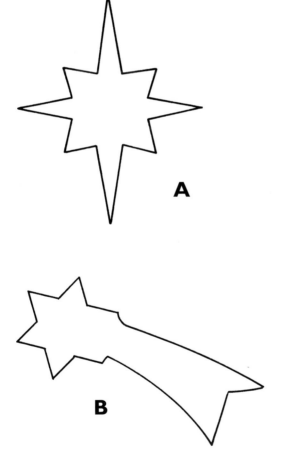

Page 111 Stars and stripes (2)

Page 101 Star of wonder

Craft suppliers

AUSTRALIA
Australia Craft Network
PO Box 350
Narellan
NSW 2567
Tel: +61 (02) 4647 7047
Fax: +61 (02) 8572 8256
www.auscraftnet.com

NEW ZEALAND
Zigzag Polymer Clay Supplies, Ltd
8 Cherry Place
Casebrook
Christchurch
Tel: +64 3359 2989
Fax: +64 3359 6394
www.zigzag.co.nz

UK
Craft Crazy
2 Barley Road
Thelwall
Warrington
Cheshire WA4 2EZ
Tel: +44 (0)1925 263263
www.craftcrazy.co.uk

Hobbycraft
The Arts and Crafts Superstore
Freephone: +44 (0)800 027 2387
www.hobbycraft.co.uk

Staedtler (UK) Ltd
Pontyclun
Rhondda Cyon Taff
CF72 8YJ
Tel: +44 (0)1443 237421
Fax: +44 (0)1443 237440
Email: salesuk@staedtler.co.uk
www.staedtler.co.uk

Studio Arts
50 North Road
Lancaster LA1 1LT
Tel: +44 (0)1524 68014
Fax: +44 (0)1524 68013
www.studioarts.co.uk

The Polymer Clay Pit
3 Harts Lane
Wortham
Diss
Norfolk IP22 1PQ
Tel/Fax: +44 (0)1379 890176
www.polymerclaypit.co.uk

USA
Big Ceramic Store
45278 Industrial Drive
Fremont
CA 94538
www.bigceramicstore.com

Factory Direct Craft Supply, Inc
315 Conover Drive
Franklin
Ohio
45005
(US customers)
Tel: +1 800 252 5223
Fax: +1 800 269 8745
(International customers)
Tel: +1 937 743 5855
Fax: +1 937 743 5500
email: krafts2u@aol.com
www.factorydirectcraft.com

Fimo Zone
Tel: +1 800 989 2889
Email: b@fimozone.com
www.fimozone.com

Polymer Clay Express
The Artway Studio
13017 Wisteria Drive
Cox 275
Germantown
MD20874
Tel: +301 482 0435
Fax: +301 482 0610
Email:
info@polymerclayexpress.com
www.polymerclayexpress.com

Wee Folk Creations
18476 Natchez Avenue
Prior Lake
MN55372
Tel: +1 952 447 3828
Fax: +1 952 447 8816
www.weefolk.com

About the author

After gaining a college qualification, Jacqui spent many years working as a graphic artist. She is now a housewife and mother to one little girl.

From an early age, Jacqui has enjoyed modelling with clay and gains much of her inspiration from wildlife. She now dedicates her spare time to creating appealing clay characters to incorporate into her card-making, a pastime that Jacqui not only finds great fun but also very rewarding.

Index

GARDENING

PHOTOGRAPHY

How to Photograph Pets	Nick Ridley
In my Mind's Eye: Seeing in Black and White	Charlie Waite
Life in the Wild: A Photographer's Year	Andy Rouse
Light in the Landscape: A Photographer's Year	Peter Watson
Photographers on Location with Charlie Waite	Charlie Waite
Photographing Wilderness	Jason Friend
Photographing your Garden	Gail Harland
Photography for the Naturalist	Mark Lucock
Photojournalism: An Essential Guide	David Herrod
Professional Landscape and Environmental Photography:	
From 35mm to Large Format	Mark Lucock
Rangefinder	Roger Hicks & Frances Schultz
Underwater Photography	Paul Kay
Where and How to Photograph Wildlife	Peter Evans
Wildlife Photography Workshops	Steve & Ann Toon

ART TECHNIQUES

Beginning Watercolours	Bee Morrison
Oil Paintings from the Landscape: A Guide for Beginners	
	Rachel Shirley
Oil Paintings from your Garden: A Guide for Beginners	
	Rachel Shirley
Sketching Landscapes in Pen and Pencil	Joyce Percival

VIDEOS

Drop-in and Pinstuffed Seats	David James
Stuffover Upholstery	David James
Elliptical Turning	David Springett
Woodturning Wizardry	David Springett
Turning Between Centres: The Basics	Dennis White
Turning Bowls	Dennis White
Boxes, Goblets and Screw Threads	Dennis White
Novelties and Projects	Dennis White
Classic Profiles	Dennis White
Twists and Advanced Turning	Dennis White
Sharpening the Professional Way	Jim Kingshott
Sharpening Turning & Carving Tools	Jim Kingshott
Bowl Turning	John Jordan
Hollow Turning	John Jordan
Woodturning: A Foundation Course	Keith Rowley
Carving a Figure: The Female Form	Ray Gonzalez
The Router: A Beginner's Guide	Alan Goodsell
The Scroll Saw: A Beginner's Guide	John Burke

MAGAZINES

WOODTURNING

WOODCARVING

FURNITURE & CABINETMAKING

THE ROUTER

NEW WOODWORKING

THE DOLLS' HOUSE MAGAZINE

OUTDOOR PHOTOGRAPHY

BLACK & WHITE PHOTOGRAPHY

KNITTING

GUILD NEWS

The above represents a full list of all titles currently published or scheduled to be published.
All are available direct from the Publishers or through bookshops, newsagents and specialist retailers.

To place an order, or to obtain a complete catalogue, contact:

**GMC Publications,
Castle Place, 166 High Street, Lewes,
East Sussex BN7 1XU United Kingdom
Tel: 01273 488005 Fax: 01273 402866**

E-mail: pubs@thegmcgroup.com

Orders by credit card are accepted